HEALING OF BROKEN FOUNDATIONS

Beth Saxen

ISBN (Paperback): 979-8-9895026-1-5
ISBN (eBook): 979-8-9895026-0-8

Foreword

In the quiet recesses of our lives lie the fragments of our past, the echoes of forgotten pains, and the shadows of childhood traumas that have shaped us in ways we might not fully comprehend. These fractures, these cracks in the foundation of our being, have a way of echoing through the years, affecting the way we relate to ourselves, to others, and even to our faith. They hinder our growth, cloud our understanding, and obscure the path toward true healing.

"Healing of Broken Foundations" is a profoundly illuminating journey into the heart of these fractures, guided by the compassionate voice of Beth Saxen. In a world where the weight of our past can become a stumbling block to our present and future, Beth brings a message of hope and renewal. Drawing from her own remarkable experiences and the wisdom she gleaned from seventeen years of ministry in the Healing Rooms of Brisbane, Beth extends her hand to all those who have ever felt the ache of unhealed wounds.

In these pages, you will discover a unique blend of personal testimony and scriptural insight, where the sacred meets the intimate struggles of the human soul. Beth deftly intertwines her own story with timeless truth, offering a tapestry of understanding for anyone who has grappled with the haunting aftermath of childhood trauma. With her gift of discernment, she unveils the intricacies of the healing process, revealing how the power of God can be a beacon of light in the darkest corners of our lives.

This book is not merely a collection of words on pages; it is a transformative tool that has the potential to mend what was shattered, strengthen what was weakened, and lead us from a place of brokenness to a place of wholeness. Becoming a Christian is indeed a transformative process; Jesus wanted us changed from the heart out. Beth's writing gives that opportunity through the healing process where we get to partner with God's Spirit as He leads us through the journey of transformation. Her insights will speak to parents navigating the challenges of nurturing their children, and to men and women alike who are seeking restoration.

As you immerse yourself in the pages of "Healing of Broken Foundations", be prepared to encounter moments of epiphany – those profound revelations that stir the soul and open the door to deep and lasting change. Beth's writing is a testament to the resiliency of the human spirit and the boundless grace of a God who yearns to mend what is broken within us.

So, whether you're wrestling with your own scars or walking alongside others in their journey toward healing, this book offers wisdom, guidance, and the assurance that broken foundations can indeed be rebuilt. May you find solace, illumination, and renewed hope within these pages, as Beth Saxen shares her heart and her faith, inviting us all to experience the transformative power of God's healing grace.

Pastor Steven Thomas
Post Graduate in Creative Writing
Masters Creative Arts

Testimonials

I have known Beth Saxen for about seventeen years now. When I first met Beth, she was on her healing journey and as she gained knowledge and understanding of inner healing she joined our team at the Logan Healing Rooms.

She has become an important team member who is trustworthy, reliable, and honest. She is kind and compassionate towards others as they seek freedom in Jesus. Beth is always willing to help and is generous with her time and resources. She is a woman of integrity and empathy.

Beth's healing journey has become a quest that has given her much insight which she has crafted into this book. This is proof of her generosity in wanting to share this road to freedom with others.

It is a pleasure to honour Beth and I commend her for writing this book.

Phil Griffith-Leake
President, Logan Healing Rooms
4 October 2023

Beth has ministered with me in the Logan Healing Rooms for over sixteen years. As well as her willingness to go on her own journey. Beth has ministered healing to hundreds of people over those years. Her ministry gift comes from hearing and following the Holy Spirit's direction and delivering that in a gentle and sensitive manner to our clients.

I also have personally been the recipient of Beth's beautiful ministry. She is not only a woman of the Word of God, but she is also constantly reading, learning, and utilising knowledge for healing from those who have long experience in this field. She is well qualified to write on this subject and I recommend her book to you.

Marian Dyer
(Co Director, Logan Healing Rooms)

Acknowledgements

Many thanks are due to Healing Room Directors Marian and Wayner Dyer for their great help in the original proof-reading of this manuscript. I am so grateful for their advice and encouragement.

Also, to Philomena Griffith-Leake, President of Logan Healing Rooms for her words of encouragement and input over the years.

Thanks also to Pastor Stephen Thomas for the generous foreword and advice.

From the Author

How exciting to be releasing my first book in the 50th year of my walk with God. Through the years I've enjoyed doing women's ministry in several churches as well as working on pastoral care teams.

I've also been involved with hospital chaplaincy as well as pastoral care in aged care residences. I'm so grateful that God could use me to help others while I have been in the process of personal healing.

By sharing about my healing journey with God, it is my hope that many people can benefit from all the things that I have learned through my struggles due to broken foundations. Thank God that He does not waste anything in our lives. Whatever tests we may go through, He will journey with us and invariably turn that test into a testimony.

However, if we desire to be the overcomers that He wants us to be, we need to be proactive in seeking our own recovery. We cannot remain passive and think that God will wave His "magic wand" over us and all will be instantly fixed. We will also need the help of others who are trained and anointed for healing ministry.

Christ said, "ask and you will receive, seek and you will find, knock and the door will be opened to you".

Hebrews 11:6 tells us, "He is a rewarder of those who diligently seek Him".

There are times that we are driven into God because of our need and in that seeking we not only find answers but also encounter Him in a way that we may never have without our trials.

John 15: 16 Jesus said, "You did not choose me, but I chose you and appointed you so that you might go and bear fruit—fruit that will last—and so that whatever you ask in my name the Father will give you".

While unresolved wounds and personal identity and relational issues remain within us, we cannot bear the beautiful fruit that He desires for us. However, He knows everything about us and with love, grace, and acceptance He will walk each of us through our journey to recovery.

Success is not a straight line. It can be two steps forward and one step backward butbe assured; He is ever-loving and patient with us on our journey.

Blessings,
Beth Saxen

Table of Contents

Healing of Broken Foundations

Beth Saxen

CHAPTER ONE

Introduction

One day, as a very new Christian, the Lord dropped four words into my spirit. They were, "Jesus breaks every fetter". In truth, I didn't even know what a fetter was, so I looked it up in Webster's dictionary and the definition was, *"A chain or shackle, something that confines or restrains you"*. At that stage of my life, I had no idea of the significance of what those words would mean to me in the coming years. Nor did I have any comprehension of the amount of emotional damage that I had accumulated during my childhood or of how many strongholds the enemy held within my soul realm.

I gave my heart to the Lord at a large Assembly of God church when I was fifteen years old and at that point, I felt such a strong presence of God about me and began an amazing love walk with Him. I believe that God gave me an accelerated growth spurt at that time because there were situations up ahead that I would need to face, and I needed to be strongly rooted in Him.

I had a very strong focus on God and His word and used to spend time writing out scriptures and getting the word deep into my heart. I was very involved in the church and went to a youth group on Saturday nights and joined the choir.

At some point, I was given solo parts in the choir which then led to doing solos during the service on Sunday nights. The music director favoured me as I believe she saw my strong dedication to the Lord. Eventually, I was involved with a Christian girl band, and we ministered in a few different places over the years. The church also did an annual music production as an outreach to the community in which I often held a prominent place. I was also asked to sing at many people's weddings. I was working as well so my life was quite full at that time.

I got married at the age of twenty and continued to work and be involved in church life. Then, at the age of twenty-eight, I had my first gorgeous son. I had stopped working at that time and stayed home with my baby, then I had two more children over the next three years so at that point, I had three children under four years of age.

Naturally, with the little ones, many of my activities stopped. I chose to go to a smaller church that was much nearer home as the one I'd attended was quite a distance away.

All my involvement with outside things stopped and as much as I loved my children, I felt like I was in a desert with constant demand and a great deal of pressure. Adding to that was the loss of sleep, constant tiredness, and no personal downtime. My husband had a very responsible job, which meant that he worked long hours.

I became very lonely and fatigued. I struggled with anxiety about how I was going to cope with everything and over time, the stress of all this triggered PTSD from my childhood.

As I progressed through life, I gradually became aware of a lot of personal issues that I struggled with, but I had no idea where they came from or how to deal with them. I had the opportunity to occasionally have a ministry here and there throughout my walk with God, however, the small amount of recovery didn't outweigh the damage and captivity that had accumulated within my soul during my childhood.

Though much of childhood was relatively normal, at the age of two, my parents, through no fault of their own, had to put my sister and me into a children's home for some time, and through this occurrence, I experienced trauma, rejection, and abandonment. When childhood security and bonding with parents is interrupted through parental loss or absence at an early age, this trauma can create within a child's soul a 'disconnect' from others and they can lack the ability to bond with other people later in life.

I also experienced repeated trauma and violation by a family member throughout my childhood years that left me with shame, intimidation, and fear of men. This kind of trauma leaves a child with a low sense of self-esteem and makes them believe that they have no rights, particularly in voicing their opinions or needs. This is why it frequently takes people many years after a traumatic childhood event to eventually voice what had happened to them way back then. Violation and intimidation will shut a person's voice down. Because of emotional wounding and lack of emotional nurture, I grew up with no sense of identity, having rights, or being valued or loved.

Though my basic physical needs were met as a child, many of my emotional needs were not. Every child has a right to feel safe, loved, and secure in their own home. If this doesn't occur and we lack a fundamental sense of protection, it makes us become very defensive and sets up within us an expectation of danger or unkindness which in turn can open us up to a spirit of negativity and evil foreboding.

My mother loved us and looked after us well, but she wasn't really an emotional nurturer. I don't remember being hugged, kissed, or hearing words of validation when I was growing up. Sadly, my father had a very dysfunctional childhood and was not capable of being relational in any way.

Many times, I felt judged and criticized both by my peers and family members. This type of environment can leave a child feeling crushed. When our 'emotional tank' is left empty as children, we do not have the emotional reserves to cope with the unkindness of people later in life.

I am very grateful that my mother sent me to Sunday school which gave me a good basic grounding in my faith, and I always had a strong consciousness of God. So, when I had an opportunity to accept Christ as Saviour at the age of fifteen, that seed of faith that had been planted in me as a young child was able to be activated into a wonderful relationship with Him. I had been born again by His Spirit and experienced a wonderful connection to Him.

While my circumstances had been positive in the early years of my salvation, I wasn't aware of how many deficits and soul wounds I was carrying. But once circumstances changed dramatically and extreme pressures came upon me, I began to see the cracks in my foundations.

God is all about relationships and He has created all people with the need to function relationally and to bond and connect to Himself and others. The enemy, however, will always seek to create strongholds within a person's life at any point of trauma, pain, or deep deficit. Demonic strongholds such as these are like stones that become 'set' in the very foundation of a person's soul. Lack of emotional nurture will in turn leave gaps in our foundations that can leave us vulnerable to anxiety, fear, and addictive behaviour.

Because of emotional wounding and brokenness, I felt unloved and found it hard to believe that I was particularly loveable either. I always felt that I had to perform and try to be perfect so that people would love me, but this never worked for me either. Also, because I was a Christian, I also believed that I had to be "nice", which meant that when people were unkind to me, I didn't feel that I had the right to speak up for myself. This created a lot of repressed anger.

As these wounds and attitudes accumulated over time and because of my issues, people didn't particularly choose me as a friend, and many Christian people without invitation, tried to "fix" me without having any knowledge or understanding of what had happened to me in my past. Consequently, it seemed to me that someone was still always telling me what was wrong with me and trying to give me trite solutions, which were shallow and erroneous, for deep problems. I was already hypersensitive to criticism so, as a result, all that these people succeeded in doing was to make me feel that everyone saw me as an inferior Christian and therefore I felt judged and resentful. I already lacked a good sense of identity or self-esteem, so these "interventions" by others only resulted in wounding me further. Because my voice had been shut down through childhood abuse, I couldn't respond to those people in a proactive way at the time that this happened.

People didn't always choose to remain friends with me and often judged me and acted superior to me because of my problems, so I became very lonely and experienced further rejection and abandonment. After years of accumulating a great deal of emotional hurt and pain, I had such a sense of grief and disappointment in life that I became chronically fatigued and struggled with digestive disorders, and my life and fruitfulness were sidelined for a number of years. Thankfully, God has a plan and purpose for us in every season and He uses those times of being sidelined to bring healing and to draw us into a deeper relationship with Himself. He also uses these times to prepare us for future ministry.

As I was unable to work due to fatigue, I had a lot of time on my hands, so I spent a great deal of that time seeking God. I also developed a skill in spiritual warfare in terms of circumstances in my life and for my family and others, though at this point, I didn't really understand or discern what my real soul issues were or how to apply that prayer and warfare to those deep wounds and demonic strongholds.

I was a diligent Christian who went to church regularly, consistently read the Word, was always honest, and had a very strong moral compass. Externally, if you'd looked at my life you would have thought that everything was just fine, but the reality was, I was very broken and in bondage and had a lot of very ungodly attitudes that had been forged by the instability of my foundational years. It wasn't until many years later, I found the organization,* International Healing Rooms, and started to go there consistently for ministry that I began a journey of recovery that is still in progress to this day.

God has done amazing things for me through consistently receiving Healing Rooms ministry and He has given me keys to apply in my own personal time with Him that has brought many breakthroughs from strongholds from my past. He has also restored my physical health in many areas. This process has enhanced my ability to understand and minister to others who are broken.

At this place in time, I have worked as a facilitator with International Healing Rooms for approximately seventeen years, and, as I said, having gone there initially to receive ministry, I also began ministering there shortly after connecting with them. I am passionate about seeing people come into wholeness and fullness of life and seeing the fruit and the power of the Spirit expressed through their lives. My hope in writing this book is to help people who have been wounded or traumatized, particularly in early childhood, and to bring understanding as to the effect that this has on an individual and how strongholds are forged within the soul at an early age. I would like to share the keys that I have found to help those who are struggling in life with the ongoing issues that result from these broken foundations.

---

* **Healing Rooms, officially registered as Healing Rooms Ministries and the Association of Healing Rooms (IAHR) is a nonprofit organization headquartered in Spokane, Washington, United States.**

CHAPTER TWO

Shaky Foundations

Some years ago, our City Council decided to extend the City Hall by digging down through the basement floors to create more underground rooms. After they began the initial digging to underpin the foundations of the building, they discovered that most of the older, original foundations were severely eroded and diminished. It turned out that years ago when the original foundations were being laid, the builders had used the water from the nearby river to mix with the cement to form the concrete footings. As the vegetation and animal organisms from the river water broke down and decomposed, this released methane gas into the concrete structure thereby compromising the integrity of the concrete. They called it "cancerous concrete". With shaky foundations, the building was in danger of sinking unevenly, cracking, or moving.

Our foundational years play such an important part in shaping our personalities, our identity, and the way that we see God, ourselves, and others. When our foundations lack the security and bonding that a child needs with their parents and others, we can struggle with feeling disconnected from life and other people. This can lead to problems with isolation, depression, and anxiety. It can also affect the way we think others see us too. God is intensely interested and invested in repairing the negative effects of our wrong foundations. He speaks in Isaiah 54 of the need to restore our foundations and to shore up those places where we have been shaken and broken and where we have not found solace or comfort. His heart is to restore us from all the effects of sin, trauma, neglect, and even generational iniquity that are passed down to us through our DNA from our family bloodline.

> Isaiah 54:10-12 (NIV) *"Though the mountains be shaken and the hills be removed, yet my unfailing love for you will not be shaken nor my covenant of peace be removed,"* says the Lord, who has compassion on you. 11 *"Afflicted city, lashed by storms and not comforted, I will rebuild you with stones of turquoise,* **your foundations** *(emphasis mine) with lapis lazuli. 12 I will make your battlements of rubies, your gates of sparkling jewels, and all your walls of precious stones".*

You can see from this passage that the will of the Father is to reinforce our foundations and our walls and to stabilize us so that we will become like the man who built his house upon the rock. When the storms came, he was not greatly moved. (Matt. 7:24-27)

To come to wholeness from broken foundational issues, we need to understand the nature of man and how we are affected by past issues. We also need to be aware of the way that demonic powers will attach themselves to wounds from the past. Wounds and trauma can create a "fracture" in the soul leaving an opening for the enemy to form strongholds that affect our thought and behavioral patterns or reactions and perceptions. These are like blocks that have been set into our soul realm. These strongholds can not only be formed from a very early age but even within the womb.

Oftentimes, we are not even aware of them, so it takes the revelation of the Holy Spirit to reveal these things to us. When

Jesus said that He heals the broken heart AND sets the captive free, (*Isaiah 61:1*), He was referring to the fact that soul wounds and brokenness leave us vulnerable to the captivity of the enemy not only when they occur in childhood, but at any stage in life. He was saying that we haven't just been hurt by things in life, but the enemy has formed a "prison" about those areas of the soul realm. This stops us from fulfilling our potential in life.

Nature of humanity

In recent years, we have had much teaching on the fact that we, as human beings, are three-part beings consisting of body, soul, and spirit. In the beginning, when God created us, He formed us from clay and then breathed His breath of life into that clay and man became a living human being. What sort of life did He breathe? Spirit life, for God, is a Spirit Being.

John 4:24 (NIV) *"God is spirit, and his worshippers must worship in the Spirit and in truth."*

So, the breath of his spirit "birthed" a living, breathing human being. This being was tri-dimensional just as God is. He is Father, Son, and Holy Spirit. We were made body, soul, and spirit.

Our Spirit's life and connection with God were like an umbilical cord that connected us to Himself and His righteousness and purity. His Spirit life governed and sustained our bodies and our soul realm. Just as a child within the womb receives all its nourishment from its connection to the mother through the umbilical cord, so we were connected to God. Another example can be an astronaut who may need to leave the spacecraft to do external repairs to the spacecraft. He is insulated within a special suit and there is a tube in the suit connecting his life supply to the ship. If that were to break, He would float away and become lost in space. Orphaned from the mothership.

When man fell from grace, he lost his spiritual connection to God leaving him with only his body and soul to use in discernment of good and evil. Basically, man was left to be controlled by his own thoughts, impulses, feelings, and desires without the moral influence and guidance of God's Spirit.

The soul consists of our mind, will, and emotions. Without our connection to the Spirit of God, we develop an orphan spirit. Fear and personal need can drive us to provide and protect ourselves without the moral conscience of the Spirit of God.

Sin and rebellion immediately brought shame and fear into Adam and Eve's souls. Because of the decision that they made to rebel against God's direction, their spirit became disconnected from God, and by this rebellion, they wounded themselves in their soul realm. They also opened a door for the enemy to have access to them and their offspring.

Eve, the mother of creation, had entered into an agreement with the serpent when he deceived her, thereby establishing a heritage for mankind that would perpetuate itself throughout future generations. At this point, man's God-given dominion over the earth had been transferred from mankind to Satan because of the misuse of man's free will. Scripture now refers to Satan as the "prince of the power of the air".

Ephesians 2:1-2 (NIV) *"As for you, you were dead in your transgressions and sins, 2 in which you used to live when you followed the ways of this world and of the ruler of the kingdom of the air, the spirit who is now at work in those who are disobedient".*

Now every day, we face the choice, do I agree with God, or do I align my thinking and behaviour with the enemy?

Amos 3:3 (KJV) says, *"Can two walk together, except they be agreed"?*

Even after we become Christians, the choices that we make in our attitudes and actions can bring us into agreement with the enemy or we can choose to agree with the Spirit of God in varying areas of our lives. Whichever one we agree with will have dominion in that area of agreement in our lives.

Our soul realm is a bit like a building. Some of the rooms or compartments are healthy and strong, some may be a bit messy, and others may be completely derelict. Things happen to us in life that wound us. We can choose to respond by the Spirit of God or from our old nature to those hurts. Our responses will give either God or the enemy access to those various compartments of our soul realm.

When children experience hurt and trauma, they are not mature enough to make proactive choices in their response to the negative things that happen to them. Therefore, they can accumulate a lot of layers of hurt, anger, bitterness, and resentment and this brings captivity to their soul realm and will seriously affect them later in life. Our negative, sinful responses and agreements with the enemy are just as wounding to our souls as was the original hurt.

Thank God that He had a redemptive plan to deliver us, from the consequences of the agreement that Eve, the mother of mankind had made with Satan.

When man fell from grace in the garden, God promised him that in the future a Messiah or Saviour would come to deliver him. His plan was to restore His Spirit of Sonship within us, thereby reawakening us spiritually into a new connection with Himself. His plan of salvation was to heal our bodies and souls and to deliver us from the dominion of the enemy which was given over to Satan by Adam and Eves' wrong choice in the garden.

> Genesis 3:15 (NIV) *"And I will put enmity between you and the woman, (Eve) and between your offspring and hers; he will **crush** your head, and you will strike (**or bruise**) his heel. "* (emphasis mine)

When God declares that one of Eves' future offspring will come and crush the head of the serpent, He is referring to the Messiah, Jesus Christ. He would be born as a man who would be "bruised" (at the cross) to "crush" the captivity of the enemy through the power of His death and resurrection. Christ took back the dominion of the enemy to bring freedom to those who receive Him. The promise was that He would bring us into a new kingdom, one that is under the Lordship of Christ so that even though we are still living in a world where demonic spirits reign, we are no longer of this world. God said that though Eve had made an agreement or alliance with the enemy, He would put enmity between the serpent and the woman and her future offspring.

Scripture tells us that unredeemed mankind is spiritually dead in sins and trespasses (Ephesians 2:1), and that it is only through Christ entering into our hearts and bringing the new birth, that we can be saved and reconnected to Him. We must receive Christ's Spirit into our hearts to become children of God. We must be born again. Just as a man and a woman's seed coming together brings natural life into fruition, even so, God's seed, which is Spirit, not flesh, must be breathed afresh into a man's heart to bring new life. It is only by the indwelling Spirit of God that we can be transformed and healed.

> John 1: 11-13 (NIV) *"He came to that which was his own, but his own did not receive him. 12 Yet to all who did receive him, (emphasis mine) to those who believed in his name, he gave the right to become children of God—13 children born not of natural descent, nor of human decision or a husband's will, but born of God"*.

CHAPTER THREE

New Beginnings

Though we were orphaned at the point of Adam and Eve's deception, through the new birth, God reconnects us to Himself by His indwelling Spirit and we receive the covenant and spirit of sonship, not because of our own righteousness, but because of the sacrifice of His Son upon the cross. We become children of God and are translated into His kingdom.

The new birth is the starting point of inner healing because it is the Spirit of God who transforms us internally.

In the Old Testament, God's Spirit came **upon** people to strengthen them and to enable them to fulfill His purposes. The Spirit of God would fall upon people so that they would prophesy or perform miracles and then He would lift off them. This was a *'visitation'* of God upon His people. However, in the New Testament culture, we have become the *'habitation'* of God's Spirit, a place where His Spirit constantly abides. God referred to this future relationship with Him in Ezekiel 36:26 (NIV) *"I will give you a new heart and put a new spirit in you; I will remove from you your heart of stone and give you a heart of flesh"*.

God has **quickened** us by His indwelling Spirit to enable us to be overcomers in all of life's situations. He wants us to walk in the newness of life.

> *intransitive verb. 1: to quicken something. 2: to come to life, especially: to enter into a phase of active growth and development, seeds quickening in the soil.* (**Webster's Dictionary**)

> Ephesians 2:1-3 (KJV) *"And you hath he quickened, who were dead in trespasses and sins; 2 Wherein in time past ye walked according to the course of this world, according to the prince of the power of the air, the spirit that now worketh in the children of disobedience: 3 Among whom also we all had our conversation in times past in the lusts of our flesh, fulfilling the desires of the flesh and of the mind; and were by nature the children of wrath, even as others"*.

So, once we are born again, we have the Spirit of God residing within us to help and strengthen us to overcome the world, our flesh, (soul realm), and the devil. However, scripture makes it clear that we can still follow the flesh, or the voice of the enemy if we choose to do so. God's desire is that we follow the direction of the abiding Spirit of God.

> Galatians 6:8 (NIV) *"Whoever sows to please their flesh, from the flesh will reap destruction; whoever sows to please the Spirit, from the Spirit will reap eternal life"*.

Choices

When it comes to our choices it's all about good fruit or bad fruit. Whatever we sow we will reap. While our spirit is born again the flesh needs to be brought into submission to Christ's work upon the cross and to the transforming power of the Holy Spirit. This process can be like a tug-of-war. The Apostle Paul spoke about this internal struggle. He says in Romans 7:15-25 (NIV).

"15 I do not understand what I do. For what I want to do I do not do, but what I hate I do. 16 And if I do what I do not want to do, I agree that the law is good. 17 As it is, it is no longer I myself who do it, but it is sin living in me. 18 For I know that good itself does not dwell in me, that is, in my sinful nature. For I have the desire to do what is good, but I cannot carry it out. 19 For I do not do the good I want to do, but the evil I do not want to do—this I keep on doing. 20 Now if I do what I do not want to do, it is no longer I who do it, but it is sin living in me that does it. 21 So I find this law at work: "Although I want to do good, evil is right there with me. 22 For in my inner being I delight in God's law; 23 but I see another law at work in me, waging war against the law of my mind and making me a prisoner of the law of sin at work within me. 24 What a wretched man I am! Who will rescue me from this body that is subject to death? 25 Thanks be to God, who delivers me through Jesus Christ our Lord! So then, I myself in my mind am a slave to God's law, but in my sinful nature a slave to the law of sin".

Note in verse 25 it says, 'Thanks be to God, who delivers me through Jesus Christ our Lord'! Christ died to give us victory and freedom over our sinful nature and demonic influence, however, our victory takes time to reclaim. The degree of an individual's struggle with the soul realm can differ greatly from one person to another, depending upon whether they had reasonably stable, loving foundations or whether those foundations were broken or traumatic. The effect of trauma from our childhood years will also vary from person to person, depending upon the frequency and intensity of the abusive episodes that happened to us back then.

Our battle as individuals is also influenced by the level of emotional neglect **and** deficits that affect a person's soul. It can take a long time to identify our own personal issues, but God will reveal things to us and work with us at a pace that we can handle. God does not show us everything at once because we would be overwhelmed by it all.

Christ overcame these things at the cross, and we as Christians must continually enforce that defeat as we become aware of our own personal issues.

God has a new inheritance, a Promised Land for each of us to possess as we progressively learn to walk in the Spirit and not according to our soul (old nature).

Galatians 5:16 (NIV) *" So I say, walk by the Spirit, and you will not gratify the desires of the flesh. 17 For the flesh desires what is contrary to the Spirit, and the Spirit what is contrary to the flesh. They are in conflict with each other, so that you are not to do whatever you want. 18 But if you are led by the Spirit, you are not under the law ".*

CHAPTER FOUR

Possessing The Blessing

The book of Joshua, in the Old Testament is an account of where Joshua leads the people of God into the Promised Land. The Promised Land is a "type" of the Spirit-filled Christian life. God had brought His people out from slavery in Egypt (which represents our old life) and led by Moses, he took them on a journey through a desert for forty years. This was a time of process for His people to prepare them to enter their promised inheritance.

Moses passed away and then Joshua was appointed to take the Children of Israel in to possess the Promised Land. However, when Joshua sent out spies to survey the land, they found that there were giants occupying the ground that had been allotted to God's people. These giants needed to be dispossessed before God's people could possess their land, and that meant that the only way to claim their inheritance was to wage war with their enemies and defeat them.

We, as Christians, must 'possess' the promised freedom and victory that is ours through Christ's sacrifice upon the cross for though our spirits are redeemed and made new at conversion, the soul realm then needs to become realigned to the new Spirit within us. The Promised Land was referred to as a land flowing with milk and honey and this land was filled with amazing fruit and provision.

This is an analogy of living in the fullness of the Spirit-filled life in Christ and of the wonderful fruits that are our inheritance in Him.

To understand our own personal 'giants', we need to look at our foundational, formative years; those who were our chief role models in life, and the way in which they and we were molded.

We do not look at our parents or forebears to in any way condemn or accuse them but rather to understand our past and forgive those who hurt us. This helps us to deal with the past and move into a healthy future.

> Isaiah 51:1-3 (NIV) *"Listen to me, you who pursue righteousness and who seek the Lord: Look to the rock from which you were cut and to the quarry from which you were hewn; 2 look to Abraham, your father, and to Sarah, who gave you birth. When I called him he was only one man, and I blessed him and made him many. 3 The Lord will surely comfort Zion and will look with compassion on all her ruins; he will make her deserts like Eden, her wastelands like the garden of the Lord. Joy and gladness will be found in her, thanksgiving and the sound of singing."*

When Isaiah says, "Look to the rock from which you were hewn", he's referring to the place that molded and fashioned us, which is our family foundation. We receive all sorts of character traits, some good and some bad, from our parental and generational influences. Often, we can recognise where our own gifts, talents, insecurities, fears, and reactions have sprung from in relation to our ancestry.

Note that in verse 2 Isaiah says, "Look to Abraham, your father, and to Sarah who gave you birth". Because we as Christians, have had two births, the natural birth, and the spiritual rebirth. This gives us a direction to our past and our future. We look behind to gain an understanding of where our negative programming came from, but we also look forward to the restoration that is ours by the Spirit of God. Note also in verse 3, God promises that He will look with compassion on our ruins and that He will make our deserts like Eden.

God first gave His covenant of blessing and prosperity to Abraham with the view that there would be a long line of descendants who would be blessed and covered by this covenant. He originally gave this promise to Abraham and his natural offspring, but He also intended to eventually bring the Gentiles to Himself through Christ so that they could become part of Abraham's lineage and heritage by faith. Through their unbelief in Christ, many of Abraham's descendants failed to receive His promised salvation, but this opened the door for the Gentiles to receive God into their hearts and to be grafted into God's own family.

Paul, referring to this blessing for the Gentiles wrote in Romans 11: 17-24 (NIV)

17 "If some of the branches have been broken off, and you, though a wild olive shoot, have been grafted in among the others and now share in the nourishing sap from the olive root, 18 do not consider yourself to be superior to those other branches. If you do, consider this: You do not support the root, but the root supports you. 19 You will say then, "Branches were broken off so that I could be grafted in." 20 Granted. But they were broken off because of unbelief, and you stand by faith. Do not be arrogant, but tremble. 21 For if God did not spare the natural branches, he will not spare you either. 22 Consider therefore the kindness and sternness of God: sternness to those who fell, but kindness to you, provided that you continue in his kindness. Otherwise, you also will be cut off. 23 And if they do not persist in unbelief, they will be grafted in, for God is able to graft them in again. 24 After all, if you were cut out of an olive tree that is wild by nature, and contrary to nature were grafted into a cultivated olive tree, how much more readily will these, the natural branches, be grafted into their own olive tree"!

Despite our past and our current problems, when we receive Christ, we are legally given the right-standing (righteousness) with God, and this gives us a solid foundation to stand upon while we allow Him to outwork His healing and transformation in our lives. We can feel loved and accepted no matter where we are in our journey with Him.

Galatians 3:6-9 (NIV) *". . . Abraham "believed God, and it was credited to him as righteousness." 7 Understand, then, that those who have faith (in Christ) are children of Abraham. 8 Scripture foresaw that God would justify the Gentiles by faith, and announced the gospel in advance to Abraham: "All nations will be blessed through you." 9 So those who rely on faith are blessed along with Abraham, the man of faith".*

Because of this right standing and sonship that has been gifted to us, we now have an inheritance attached to this position.

Galatians 3:26-29 (NIV) *26 "So in Christ Jesus you are all children of God through faith, 27 for all of you who were baptized into Christ have clothed yourselves with Christ. 28 There is neither Jew nor Gentile, neither slave nor free, nor is there male and female, for you are all one in Christ Jesus. 29 If you belong to Christ, then you are Abraham's seed, and heirs according to the promise".*

God's desire is to love and bless all people, but those who reject His plan of salvation, remain under the curse of the enemy. This is not because God curses them, as today we are under the season of grace through the New Covenant. However, man has been given free will and authority over his own life to choose his own alliances and these choices can allow either God or Satan access into our lives.

Deuteronomy 30:19 (NIV)" *I call heaven and earth to witness against you today, that I have set before you life and death, blessing and curse. Therefore choose life, that you and your offspring may live"*

Jeremiah 17:5-8 (NIV) *"This is what the Lord says: "Cursed is the one who trusts in man, who draws strength from mere flesh and whose heart turns away from the Lord. 6 That person will be like a bush in the wastelands; they will not see prosperity when it comes. They will dwell in the parched places of the desert, in a salt land where no one lives. 7 "But blessed is the one who trusts in the Lord, whose confidence is in him. 8 They will be like a tree planted by the water that sends out its roots by the stream. It does not fear when heat comes; its leaves are always green. It has no worries in a year of drought and never fails to bear fruit."*

Not only do the choices that we make today have an impact upon us and our offspring for good or bad, but the choices that our antecedents made 'way back then' can continue to affect us. Sometimes we observe alcohol or gambling addictions which are inherited genetically through the family bloodline as well as many sicknesses and diseases.

One mother I knew had an adult son who was habitually promiscuous. This ruined his marriage, and it continues to be a stronghold in his life to this day. One day she said to me, "He's just like his father". She went on to say that she had left the father of her son when the son was in his infancy and that the father had never circumstantially been an influence in his son's life. Yet this poor young man displayed the same character defects from his paternal bloodline that were passed on to him and unfortunately, this undermined his life choices which hurt him and many others in the process.

We are all a conglomeration of genetic material that "programs" us in many, varying ways. However, we don't just inherit genetic programming that affects our physical and personality traits from our forebears but also "familiar" or family spirits can be trans-ferred from generation to generation. For some people, their good inheritance outweighs the bad and for others, it can be the opposite.

> *"Jesus spent at least a third of His time healing and casting out demons. Spirits can gain access into people or into the personalities of individuals. When there are spirits that go from generation to generation, manifesting on a piece of land, or in an actual family or bloodline, those spirits are called familiar spirits."* **https://lancewallnau.com/break-ing-off-familiar-spirits/or in an actual family or bloodline, those spirits are called familiar spirits".**

To recap, when we come to Christ, our spirit is made new and alive to God, however, our soul realm must be renewed and transformed over time. Christ paid the price at the cross to give us victory over all strongholds, sin, sickness, and generational curses, however it is up to us as Christians to enforce the defeat of the enemy through the blood of the Lamb and the resurrection power of the Spirit. Each one of us has had a cultural, spiritual, social, emotional, and financial inheritance that impacts our souls so that no matter how earnestly we follow Christ, our individual walks can be poles apart. If we have had poor, broken, damaged foundations we have much more to overcome than other Christians.

I have heard some Christians teach that we don't need emotional healing because the work was all done at the cross and all we must do is draw it up from the indwelling Spirit. But there are times when strongholds (giants) must be dispossessed before the new life can be possessed.

> Mark 3:27 *"Or how can someone enter a strong man's house and plunder his goods, unless he first binds the strong man? Then indeed he may plunder his house".*

Until the strongman is broken, no amount of confessing the Word or trying to renew our minds will be effective. It is difficult for many people to discern for themselves where their past is still affecting their present-day in a negative way. We need someone to help us who can discern by the Spirit where there are strongholds within our lives. An experienced facilitator can help bring deliverance, freedom, and healing to the places where people have been wounded and shut down.

CHAPTER FIVE

Trauma and Interaction Between Our Brain, Nervous System, and Hormonal Secretions

In dealing with the effects of deficit and trauma in a person's life, we must understand the impact of trauma upon the physical body as well as the soul. Science shows us that there are sheaths of neurons that lie in the brain, heart, spinal cord, and the gut which interconnect with and transmit impulses to each other.

Neurons are nerve cells that contain memories. Our neurological pathways as well as our soul contain memories that can hold us in bondage to painful, traumatic experiences. The internal stress created by these wounds and memories can then affect the health and chemical balance of our whole body. In understanding this, we have a clearer direction as to how to pray into the physiological effects left by trauma as well as the psychological issues. Jesus is passionate about healing people who are broken-hearted and restoring the whole person.

Let's look at how childhood trauma and inadequate protection and nurture affect the brain development of a child, as well as wounding their souls.

"Brain development is affected by stress early in development. Extensive research has been carried out on the neurobiology of stress. The link between a history of childhood abuse and neglect and neuro-endocrine impacts is well established. Research tells us that the bodies of children who are being abused react and adapt to the unpredictable dangerous environments to which they are exposed. Stress can set off a ripple of hormonal changes that permanently wire a child's brain to cope with a malevolent world. Through this chain of events, violence, and abuse pass from generation to generation (Teicher, 2002).

The neuro-endocrine system refers to the system of interaction between our brain/ nervous system and the hormones in our bodies. This system helps regulate our moods, our stress response, our immune system, and our digestion, amongst other things. Any disruption to the neuro-endocrine system affects a range of basic psychological and physiological functions. **https://www.blueknot.org.au/Workers-Practitioners/For-Health-Professionals/Resources-for-Health-Professionals/Ways-Health-Compromised**

Sometimes the effects of childhood trauma will be diagnosed as ADHD.

"About 6 million children in the U.S. have been diagnosed with attention deficit hyperactivity disorder, or ADHD. Nearly two-thirds of those kids have another mental,

emotional, or behavioral disorder as well. One of those conditions could be childhood traumatic stress.

Childhood traumatic stress is the psychological reaction that children have to a traumatic event, whether it happens to them, or they see it happen to someone else. These events can affect children's brains, emotions, and behavior in the same way traumatic events can affect adults.

Sometimes, going through a traumatic event can cause real attention problems. But trauma and ADHD can be confused in diagnosis because the symptoms of trauma mimic those of ADHD.

They share several symptoms, including:

- *Trouble concentrating*
- *Difficulty learning*
- *Easily distracted*
- *Doesn't listen well*
- *Disorganized*
- *Hyperactive/restless*
- *Doesn't sleep well*

Some studies show that children diagnosed with ADHD are more likely to have had a traumatic event than children who don't have ADHD. Scientists have also found that ADHD and childhood traumatic stress affect the same region of the brain: the prefrontal and temporal cortex, which controls emotions, impulses, and decision-making".
https://www.webmd.com/add-adhd/childhood-adhd/adhd-traumatic-childhood-stress#1

We can see from this, how childhood trauma and neglect have both a psychological and physiological impact on a human being, affecting the brain, the nervous system, the gut, and the hormonal secretions of the body. This is why people with poor foundations often must deal with chemical imbalances later in life unless they find healing and deliverance. When dealing with trauma in prayer we are not just asking God to heal and break strongholds from the mind (*which is part of our soul*) and memories, but to also heal the brain itself. The brain, on average, contains about 100 billion nerve cells called neurons. (Some scientific opinions differ slightly)

The heart is another physical organ that must be ministered to.

Effects of trauma on the heart

Science tells us that the heart possesses about forty-thousand neurons, and again, these cells contain memories. Our neurons help us to learn and retain information, and to sense and feel. There are many documented cases where heart transplant recipients have experienced their donors' memories and/or subtle changes in their personalities.

"Can An Organ Transplant Change A Recipient's Personality? Cell Memory Theory Affirms 'Yes' – Heart Transplants and Cell Memory

"The cell memory phenomenon, while still not considered 100 percent scientifically-validated, is still supported by several scientists and physicians. The behaviors and emotions acquired by the recipient from the original donor are due to the combinatorial memories stored in the neurons of the organ donated. Heart transplants are said to be the most susceptible to cell memory where organ transplant recipients experience a change of heart. The parallels that were observed in the study were changes in food, music, art, sexual, recreational, and career preferences in addition to name associations and sensory experiences. Jul 9, 2013" **https://**

www.medicaldaily.com/can-organ-transplant-change-recipients-personality-cell-memory-theory-affirms-yes-247498

Recently, I read an account of an eight-year-old girl who was a heart transplant recipient. Her organ donor was a ten-year-old girl who had been murdered. After the transplant, the girl began having recurring dreams about an actual murder. When taken to a psychiatrist he concluded that the girl was experiencing 'flashbacks' of the traumatic death of her donor. Further inquiries confirmed this, and information given to the police from these memories led to the conviction of the ten-year-old killer. **https://www.historydisclosure.com/transplant-recipients-pick-up-the-memories-of-their-donors/**

Impact of trauma upon the gut and digestive tract

Trauma is transmitted from the brain to the gut.

Scientists say that we have a second 'brain' in our gut. There is a major nerve called the Vagus nerve that runs from the center of the brain to the gut and other organs. The brain and gut have nervous systems that function autonomously, yet they are also connected by the vagus nerve which sends signals both ways. The brain is our rational processor, 'our thinking brain', however our gut, the second brain, contains approximately 100 million neurons that lie in sheaths that line our stomach, our esophagus, and our bowels. This is our emotional processor or 'feeling brain'. So, we have a reasoning and thinking brain in our head, and an emotional brain in our gut that tells our thinking brain how we feel. This is why we often say, "My head tells me to do one thing, and my gut tells me to do another".

The following information also brings understanding as to the complexity of the correlation between the brain and digestive system to light and how stress and negativity affect our bodies.

"We all talk about 'gut feelings,' but few of us really appreciate the amazingly strong connections between the brain and the digestive system. The stomach and intestines actually have more nerve cells than the entire spinal cord, leading some experts to call the digestive system a "mini-brain." A highway of nerves runs directly from the real brain to the digestive system, and messages flow in two directions. Consider this: 95 percent of the body's serotonin – a hormone that helps control mood – is found in the digestive system, not the brain.

The impact of stress on the stomach goes far beyond indigestion, however. In recent years, doctors have uncovered a remarkably complex connection between the brain and the digestive system. The entire system is extremely sensitive to our moods. In fact, experts now see stress as a major player in a wide range of digestive problems, including irritable bowel syndrome, indigestion, and heartburn". **https://consumer.healthday.com/encyclopedia/ digestive-health-14/digestion-health-news-200/stress-and- the-digestive-system-645906.html**

This article also affirms what we've just read.

"Chronic disorders of the gastrointestinal tract such as food allergies, inflammatory bowel disease (IBD), and irritable bowel syndrome (IBS) continue to impose considerable personal and social burdens worldwide. However, a detailed understanding of what causes the symptoms associated with these disorders is lacking. These diseases appear to share an exaggerated inflammatory response to an otherwise benign external stimulus, or one against which tolerance should have been developed. The mechanisms through which "initial sensitization" occurs may shed new

light on the pathophysiology of a variety of chronic gastro-intestinal disorders and pave the way toward therapeutic strategies for patients with allergic disorders.

The role of external factors, such as psychological stress, in triggering inflammatory reactions has become a topic of intense research activity. Stress may trigger allergic reactions in the gut and other organs, and depression or anxiety may worsen symptoms in inflammatory disorders of the intestine." **https://www.ncbi.nlm.nih.gov/pmc/articles/PMC1592668/**

From this information, we can see how profoundly stress can impact our digestive system and can trigger intestinal disorders. These disorders can play a major part in depression and anxiety. As we observed earlier, the greater part of our serotonin production, which is our "happy" hormone, is formed in the gut, so where there is stress and imbalance, this depletes our serotonin levels and adversely affects our sense of well-being.

Stress also affects the body's production of melatonin, which regulates our sleep-wake cycle. Disrupted sleep patterns are generally symptomatic of those whose melatonin has become depleted.

This is what you might call a vicious cycle where negative emotions impact our health and our bad health then in turn continues to impact our emotions.

"If you have been diagnosed with any type of mood disorder, then you have probably heard the word "serotonin" before. Despite being familiar with the word itself you may have asked yourself 'what is serotonin and why does it matter?' Serotonin is a brain chemical, or neurotransmitter, responsible for regulating many of the functions in your body that contribute to your overall health and wellbeing,

and people who have anxiety disorders generally do not have enough of it.

There is some debate as to whether or not serotonin is low because you have anxiety, or vice versa. However, it appears that addressing your anxiety is likely to have a positive effect on serotonin levels as well." **https://www. calmclinic.com/other/serotonin-and-anxiety**

From all of this we can see how unresolved trauma affects our digestion and chemical balance. I will give keys as to how to pray for these issues, later in the book.

CHAPTER SIX

Effect of Negative Emotions
Upon the Body and Soul

S cripture tells us in Proverbs 4:23 (NIV) *"Above all else, guard your heart, for everything you do flows from it"*.

The King James version says this, *"Keep your heart with all diligence, For out of it spring the issues of life"*.

Our life "flow" comes from our hearts, our minds, and our emotions, which in turn affect our physical bodies. When these areas are under the control of the Holy Spirit, we are healthy physically and emotionally. Wherever they are not under His control we have negative consequences. This is why we must guard and maintain our wellspring with diligence from negative or unproductive attitudes. We must also allow the Holy Spirit to help us process any anger, unforgiveness, or wounds that can happen to us daily. Unfortunately, for many people, our issues stem from things that happened to us way back in our foundational years, when we were unable to find healing or to make conscious choices relating to attitudes and alliances that were formed back then in our soul realm. The effects of these things can accumulate over the years as people may continue to hurt us in those places where we were originally wounded because these areas of past hurt are unresolved and highly sensitive.

Some believe that the center of our being where our spirit resides is in the gut area. Christ made this statement about those who would be born again by His Spirit.

> John 7:37-39 (KJV) *"In the last day, that great day of the feast, Jesus stood and cried, saying, If any man thirst, let him come unto me, and drink. 38 He that believeth on me, as the scripture hath said, out of his belly shall flow rivers of living water. 39 (But this spake he of the Spirit, which they that believe on him should receive: for the Holy Ghost was not yet given; because that Jesus was not yet glorified.)"*

Verse 39 confirms that the 'rivers of living water' relate to the flow of the Holy Spirit which we received at the point of salvation.

> *"The ancients saw the bowel as the seat of human emotion: Greek poets, from Aeschylus down, regarded the bowels as the seat of the more violent passions such as anger and love, but by the Hebrews they were seen as the seat of tender affections, especially kindness, benevolence, and compassion."* *Some early English bibles used the word bowels to mean pity or compassion. Later it was retranslated as heart. So the heart and gut have some relation. They're both internal organs associated with feelings and human depth."* **https://godinallthings.com/2012/05/21/the-heart-the-gut/**

Here are a few scripture references relating to the central core of man.

Philemon 1:7 (KJV) "For we have great joy and consolation in thy love, because the bowels of the saints are refreshed by thee, brother".

Philippians 2:1 (KJV) *" If there be therefore any consolation in Christ, if any comfort of love, if any fellowship of the Spirit, if any bowels and mercies".*

Philippians 1:8 (KJV) *"For God is my record, how greatly I long after you all in the bowels of Jesus Christ".*

Emotions affect various parts of our bodies

"Did you know that every feeling you have affects some part of your body? While positive emotions such as gratitude have been scientifically linked to a number of beneficial health effects, negative emotions, and stress can wreak havoc — especially if you're not exercising or eating right, as both of these can ease pessimism and help keep stress in check.

It's interesting to note that certain emotions are known to be associated with pain in certain regions of your body, even though science cannot explain exactly why this is. For example, those suffering from depression will often experience chest pains, even when there's nothing physically wrong with their heart. Extreme grief can also have a devastating impact, and research confirms that in the days following the loss of a loved one, your risk of suffering a heart attack increases by 21 times.

While the exact mechanics of these mind-body links are still being unraveled, what is known is that your brain, and consequently your thoughts and emotions, play a distinct role in your experience of physical pain, and can

contribute to the development of chronic disease." **https://
articles.mercola.com/sites/articles/archive/2018/05/17/effect-
of-negative-emotions-on-health.aspx**

Some years ago, a lady who had been verbally abused by her husband over many years came to Healing Rooms for prayer. When she first came, she was also suffering from a frozen shoulder. She continued coming for prayer over a period of weeks, and we led her to forgive her husband and kept praying into the wounds and trauma. We also broke off the power of negative words from her soul and neurological memories as well. After a while, not only was her soul healed, but the frozen shoulder was released into normal mobility again. This shows how our soul realm can affect our body as well.

Effects of negativity and trauma within the womb

As mentioned earlier, emotions, trauma, wounds, fears, and generational iniquity can also be passed on to us while still within the womb.

> *"Experts and evidence suggest that positive thinking can shape the body, heal internally, and even nurture a healthier child during pregnancy.*
>
> *A pregnant woman's thoughts have a physical connection to her unborn child. "Everything the pregnant mother feels and thinks is communicated through neurohormones to her unborn child, just as surely as are alcohol and nicotine," says Dr. Thomas Verny whose books, professional publications, and founding of the Association for Prenatal and Perinatal Psychology and Health (APPPAH) and Journal of Prenatal and Perinatal Psychology and Health, have established him as one of the world's leading*

authorities on the effects of prenatal environment on personality development.

A pregnant woman's thoughts are the precursor for her emotions. And her emotions are the precursor for the neurohormones that Thomas Verny refers to.

In "Magical Beginnings, Enchanted Lives," Dr. Deepak Chopra clearly explains what pregnancy research is showing, "When a pregnant mother is anxious, stressed, or in a fearful state, the stress hormones released into her bloodstream cross through the placenta to the baby. Hundreds of studies have confirmed that chemicals released by the pregnant mother's body are transported into the womb and affect the unborn baby."

Negative thoughts are often the root cause of a fear-based stress response. Chopra says, "Stress activates the unborn child's endocrine system and influences fetal brain development. Children born to mothers who had intensely stressful pregnancies are more likely to have behavioral problems later in life." Verny says, "Studies show that mothers under extreme and constant stress are more likely to have babies who are premature, lower than average in weight, hyperactive, irritable, and colicky." **https://getfit-forbirth.com/a-mothers-emotions-affect-her-unborn-child/**

Many people are affected by stress or negativity in the womb. A friend of mine shared her testimony when, as a mother who already had four children, she became quite resentful when she found herself pregnant again with a fifth child. She struggled with this throughout her pregnancy and after her son was born, she noticed that he used to frequently sob in his sleep. She shared how she repented for rejecting her child in her heart and prayed over him breaking the spirit of rejection from him. She then declared over him that she did love him and wanted him. After she did this, she said that the baby never cried in his sleep again. By her repentance and declaration, she broke something in the spirit realm over her child.

God knew us from conception, and He had a wonderful purpose and plan for our lives, but the enemy will always seek to waylay our destiny through wounding our souls at our foundational level and destroying our sense of identity and purpose if he can.

> Psalm 139:13-16 (NIV) *"For you created my inmost being; you knit me together in my mother's womb. 14 I praise you because I am fearfully and wonderfully made; your works are wonderful, I know that full well. 15 My frame was not hidden from you when I was made in the secret place, when I was woven together in the depths of the earth. 16 Your eyes saw my unformed body; all the days ordained for me were written in your book before one of them came to be".*

Often when people have had negative foundations, they can tend to blame God, yet Jesus made it clear that God is light and life and that there is no darkness in Him. He speaks about this in John 10:10 (NIV)

> *"The thief comes only to steal and kill and destroy; I have come that they may have life, and have it to the full".*

This scripture is the dividing line in the Bible regarding light and darkness. When we are in the kingdom of darkness, we are under the sway of principalities and powers, and this brings destruction. However, once we are born again, we come into God's kingdom and His desire is to heal, deliver, and restore.

Many Christians still actually believe that everything that comes into their lives is from God. We need God's discernment to direct us as to how to stand in each trial that we face in life.

Scripture tells us clearly that we are not always wrestling against flesh and blood, but with principalities and powers (Eph. 6:12-13), and in these battles we must take up the weapons of our warfare (2 Cor. 10:4).

There is no darkness in God or in heaven. Jesus taught us to pray that His kingdom would come to earth as it is in heaven.

1 John 1:5 5 (Berean) *"And this is the message we have heard from Him and announce to you: God is light, and in Him there is no darkness at all".*

Scripture tells us that we will always have trials in life but the way that we handle them will either bring good fruit and growth into our character or we can become negative and embittered. God allows testing and trials to refine us and make us more like Him. We can only improve our character if we choose the right responses to our challenges. The following scriptures show us what we should be aiming for in our attitudes as Christians.

Galatians 5:22 (NIV) *But the fruit of the Spirit is love, joy, peace, forbearance, kindness, goodness, faithfulness, 23 gentleness and self-control. Against such things there is no law.*

Let's look at the nature of God's love.

1 Corinthians 13:4 (NIV) *Love is patient, love is kind. It does not envy, it does not boast, it is not proud. 5 It does not dishonor others, it is not self-seeking, it is not easily angered, it keeps no record of wrongs. 6 Love does not delight in evil but rejoices with the truth. 7 It always protects, always trusts, always hopes, always perseveres.*

When we've had broken foundations, there will be a backlog of attitudes to be realigned. This takes time, but God knows where you came from, and He is patient and loving towards you while you are walking towards recovery.

Sometimes we can become aware of a pattern of behaviour or negative responses that seems to repeat itself within our own family. We must ask God if a door was opened to the enemy through sin or if it's attached to a wound. We also need to ask God if our descendants have done anything to allow its entrance. If He shows us something then we must ask the Spirit of God to give us keys to dismantle this.

We see the desire of God's heart for us when John prayed in 3 John 1: 2 (KJV)

"Beloved, I wish above all things that thou mayest prosper and be in health, even as thy soul prospereth".

Once the Spirit of God takes up residency within us, He enables us to overcome whatever challenges we may have from our broken foundations. We read in 2 Peter 1: 3 (NIV)

"His divine power has given us everything we need for a godly life through our knowledge of him who called us by his own glory and goodness".

CHAPTER SEVEN

Holy Spirit Brings Transformation

It is the power of the cross that helps us to overcome sinful habits and behavioral patterns and it's the **anointing** of the indwelling presence of God's Spirit who breaks ungodly yokes, sets us free from the law, and transforms us into the image of Christ.

> Isaiah 10:27 (KJV) *"And it shall come to pass in that day, that his burden shall be taken away from off thy shoulder, and his yoke from off thy neck, and the yoke shall be destroyed because of the **anointing**"*.

Many times, it takes a 'word of knowledge' given by the Holy Spirit to identify why someone is struggling in a certain area (1 Cor. 12:8).

The **anointing of the Spirit** came upon Christ in the form of a dove, after He had been baptized by John in the Jordan River (Luke 3:22). This anointing empowered Christ to commence His ministry and fulfill His mandate of salvation, healing, deliverance, and restoration.

After this experience at His water baptism Christ went to Nazareth, his hometown, and into the local synagogue to proclaim His mission statement. He stood up to read, and the scroll of the prophet Isaiah was handed to Him. Unrolling it, He found the place in Isaiah 61 (NIV) where it is written:

*"The Spirit of the Sovereign Lord is on me, because the Lord **has anointed me** (my emphasis) to proclaim good news to the poor. He has sent me to bind up the brokenhearted, to proclaim freedom for the captives and release from darkness for the prisoners,*

2 to proclaim the year of the Lord's favor and the day of vengeance of our God, to comfort all who mourn,

3 and provide for those who grieve in Zion—to bestow on them a crown of beauty instead of ashes, the oil of joy instead of mourning, and a garment of praise instead of a spirit of despair. They will be called oaks of righteousness, a planting of the Lord for the display of his splendor.

4 They will rebuild the ancient ruins and restore the places long devastated; they will renew the ruined cities that have been devastated for generations.

5 Strangers will shepherd your flocks; foreigners will work your fields and vineyards.

6 And you will be called priests of the Lord, you will be named ministers of our God. You will feed on the wealth of nations, and in their riches you will boast.

7 Instead of your shame you will receive a double portion, and instead of disgrace you will rejoice in your inheritance. And so you will inherit a double portion in your land, and everlasting joy will be yours.

8 "For I, the Lord, love justice; I hate robbery and wrongdoing. In my faithfulness I will reward my people and make an everlasting covenant with them.

9 Their descendants will be known among the nations and their offspring among the peoples. All who see them will acknowledge that they are a people the Lord has blessed."

10 I delight greatly in the Lord; my soul rejoices in my God. For he has clothed me with garments of salvation and arrayed me in a robe of his righteousness, as a bridegroom adorns his head like a priest, and as a bride adorns herself with her jewels.

11 For as the soil makes the sprout come up and a garden causes seeds to grow, so the Sovereign Lord will make righteousness and praise spring up before all nations".

From these verses of scripture, we can see how passionate God is about healing and restoring individuals and families. Later, Jesus passed His personal mandate on to His church when He said to go into the entire world and do the works that He did. Sadly, the church has concentrated on peoples' behavior and sin and has not understood the deeper issues that so many have in their lives from their past. There has been little or no understanding of how to minister to people to bring wholeness, freedom, and righteousness so that they may become the fruitful, powerful people that God intended for them to be. Thankfully, there are many good ministries available today to help those who are struggling with past issues.

People can sit in church with unresolved hurts, painful memories, and strongholds of trauma, grief, violation, abandonment, rejection, shame, and a multitude of other issues that spring from varying underlying causes, including generational curses. They can also at the same time have a lot of repressed anger, bitterness, judgement, offense, and unforgiveness in relation to those traumas, which they have been unable to process properly because of the lack of resolution to their pain. I've heard some Christian people say that if you just forgive, it will all be healed, but this is an extremely simplistic concept to think that people who have had so much brokenness and consequently have so many strongholds within their souls can make a full recovery by forgiveness alone. In fact, without healing and deliverance to deeply wounded areas, some people can find it impossible to release forgiveness to others.

I often hear motivational preachers saying things like, "Leave the past behind and walk into your future with God". That may be possible in some situations but while we are still being affected by traumatic memories, we can't just 'flick a switch' and forget the past violation.

Because trauma causes cyclic thinking, people become trapped in that cycle of negative memories held by strongholds.

Forgiveness is often a process that takes time as we repent of bad attitudes and are healed of our wounds and strongholds.

Scripture tells us that we shouldn't go to bed with anger in our hearts, because if we do we give the devil a mighty foothold in our lives. (Eph. 4:26) When children are repeatedly abused and vulnerable in their early formative years, they do not have the ability to make a conscious choice to deal with their anger or to forgive someone for that abuse. When a scenario like this is repeated over and over again, there will be multiple layers of memories that hold trauma, anger, and violation and these become 'set' in stronghold form within a growing child.

Trauma creates a wound like a 'crack" or fragmenting within the soul. This vulnerability opens the door for demonic spirits to come in and attach themselves to that wound and hold that person in bondage to the traumatic event. It's a bit like when sheep have a wound and the wound becomes 'fly-blown'. This is where flies will lay eggs that turn into maggots in the festering wound. That is the nature of a stronghold. (More about strongholds in Chapter 12).

Once deliverance ministry is applied to the memories of a fragmented soul, we need to pray for healing into the brain and heart and nervous system, asking the Holy Spirit to bring back and amalgamate all the scattered dissociated parts of a person's soul.

When people have unresolved wounds and strongholds and then later, experience some sort of violation of their rights, hurt, or abandonment, they will react out of the wellspring of hurt and anger that is already residing within them. This then causes them to accumulate more wounds in their soul until they are set free. Childhood abuse leads to feeling disempowered, developing a victim mentality, fear of man and to being easily intimidated. Sometimes conversely, it can also lead to a person becoming aggressive and violent in later years. The self-worth of a person can be damaged by words that are diminishing or cruel, being spoken over us by parental or authority figures or even our peers.

Deficits

Many people carry within them a sense of grief that their childhood lacked the nurture, security, and validation that they needed. The deficits in our upbringing can leave us with an orphan spirit or a spirit of desolation, isolation, disappointment, and loneliness. We can lack the basic building blocks that enable us to have a sense of purpose and meaningful relationships.

When we lack love and affection, we subconsciously internalize the mindset that we are not loveable, and this is a lie that we must renounce. Unfortunately, when we haven't had the healthy foundations that give us a good grounding in relationships, we can find that as we progress in life, people weigh us up and find us wanting and then marginalize us, so then we experience further isolation, rejection, and loneliness. Sadly, when this is the case, we can lack the ability to nurture the next generation well and this pattern repeats itself throughout the successive generations. This generational pattern is what verse 4 of Isaiah 61 is referring to when it says, *"they shall repair the waste cities, **the desolations of many generations**"* (emphasis mine).

Lack of emotional nurture is also a form of abuse.

What are the effects of uninvolved parents?

- Children with uninvolved parents may:
- Be anxious or stressed due to the lack of family support
- Be emotionally withdrawn
- Fear of becoming dependent on other people
- Have an increased risk of substance abuse
- Have to learn to provide for themselves
- Exhibit more delinquency during adolescence

    https://www.verywellmind.com/what-is-uninvolved-parenting-2794958#:~:text=Children%20with%20uninvolved%20parents%20may%3A%201%20Be%20anxious,for%20themselves%206%20Exhibit%20more%20delinquency%20during%20adolescence

We are wired for love. God is love and He created mankind with the intrinsic need to love and be loved. If there is an absence of demonstrative love in a child's foundations, the child will often fail to bond with their parents and will then struggle to be emotionally connected with others later in life. Because of this, they can be in a group situation but always feel "left out", not a part of things, or different from others and lonely. For some, this disconnect becomes their paradigm of normality. When this has been the case, a person may not feel the need for connective relationships with others and won't even perceive that this is a problem. We can have essential parts of our personality that are missing and not even realise it or miss it because we've never known what it is to be connected.

The London Journal of Primary Care

"Human babies are born very dependent on their parents. They undergo huge brain development, growth, and neuron pruning in the first two years of life. The brain development of infants (as well as their social, emotional, and cognitive development) depends on a loving bond or attachment relationship with a primary caregiver, usually a parent. There is increasing evidence from the fields of development psychology, neurobiology and animal epigenetic studies that neglect, parental inconsistency and a lack of love can lead to long-term mental health problems as well as to reduced overall potential and happiness". **https://www.ncbi.nlm.nih.gov/pmc/articles/PMC5330336/**

Parents are meant to be representatives of God's loving, caring nature, by providing nurture to their children, and they are responsible for laying healthy emotional foundations for them. A parent's affirmation, praise, and nurture 'initialize' or 'activate' within a child, their sense of worth, identity, and connection to others. Parents are responsible for empowering each individual child to identify his or her own gifts and talents and to allow them opportunities to explore and develop their gifts and talents as this enhances their sense of unique individuality. Grandparents also make a major contribution to the lives of their grandchildren. Children need opportunities to develop social skills and learn to interact with people of all ages. Parents also initialize initiative within a child. You often find that those who have lacked parental nurture, lack the essential initiative to explore their own gifts and talents and to be motivated to get out into society and fulfill their potential. As mentioned before, parents who have lacked those foundational building blocks themselves, lack the necessary skills that enable them to impart this to their own children.

We need to identify the deficits in our foundations that have hindered the development of our identity and potential. It takes the discernment of the Holy Spirit to recognise any stronghold spirits that have infiltrated those voids that impede our development and growth in Christ.

Mark 3:27 (NIV) *"In fact, no one can enter a strong man's house without first tying him up. Then he can plunder the strong man's house".*

Firstly, we must take the authority of Christ to the spirit of rejection, trauma, abandonment, violation, etc. (whatever the stronghold spirits are) and break them off in the name of Christ. We need to ask the Holy Spirit to heal the wounds and memories in the soul in relation to any childhood trauma or neglect, and to heal the associated cellular memories held within our neurological pathways. It's important to release forgiveness to those people who failed to nurture us in any way. We must then break off any negative words spoken over us by them and negative soul ties with them. This doesn't mean that we break all soul ties with those who hurt us, only the unproductive ones.

We then need to ask the Spirit of God to "initialize" identity and empower initiative within us so that we are motivated to use our God-given gifts and talents in life. For those areas where we have lacked bonding with parents or caregivers, it is as if our 'emotional receptors' have not been 'turned on' or 'attuned' to be connected to others. We must ask God to heal and restore the relational connections that have lain dormant within our lives and to bring us into the right relationship with God the Father, ourselves, and others.

We must repent of any sinful responses to our forebears and forgive them, asking God to cleanse and heal our souls.

This is often the hardest part of recovery because what others did to us as vulnerable children was not fair and it wasn't our fault.

However, without forgiveness, the enemy still has a right of access into your life and so this 'door' must be closed so that we can live in freedom.

If we have had a foundation of being extremely wounded and have a love deficit, negative things that people do or say to us have a much greater impact on us than someone who has a well-nurtured soul. Our capacity to forgive and respond with grace to these people can be non-existent because of our own internal love deficit. These wounds plus our sinful responses to them, can seem like a mountainous object to overcome. At times like this, I've learned to declare God's grace to those areas where I've felt so desolate and unable to have a Godly response.

Zechariah 4:7 (KJV) *"Who art thou, O great mountain? Before Zerubbabel thou shalt become a plain: and he shall bring forth the headstone thereof with shoutings, crying, Grace, grace unto it".*

I love Romans 5:20 (KJV) which says, *"But where sin abounded, grace did much more abound".* There are times when we feel "stuck" in bad attitudes. Only the spirit of God can give us the specific keys for our breakthrough.

Sometimes the enemy will keep reminding us of these past offences to keep us focused on them and in a place of striving to overcome them. We can have familiar spirits attached to memories that 'replay' hurts and events that happened to us. There are times when we must cut off soul ties to those spirits and renounce agreements that we made with them. We put off the old and then put on the new life that comes from the Spirit of God.

Over the years, I have spent many hours with the communion elements, bringing my attitudes in death to the cross by the power of Christ's broken body, asking Him to cleanse me by the blood, and then receiving the resurrection power of the Spirit to transform and heal.

It can take a long time to process forgiveness and repentance for all the ungodly attitudes that we took on board at the time of each painful occurrence. This is especially so if a person has had multiple layers of hurts in their hearts that have accumulated over a period of many years as each painful instance has its own separate memory and impact upon us. For instance, it's very rare that breaking the power of rejection over someone will cover every past memory that contains rejection. When unsure of how to pray in relation to layers of memories of hurt and trauma we can just ask the Holy Spirit, "What area do you want to heal today? Or is there a particular memory that you want to deal with at this moment"? Invariably He will reveal something from the past that needs to be healed and forgiven. It may even be a lie that we've taken on board as children. We can then renounce those things and receive His truth instead of the lie.

We cannot minister healing to others just by methods. Operating in this gift must come from a relationship with Christ whereby we hear the voice and direction of the Spirit of God and operate in submission to Him. Not everyone can operate in this gift.

The initial time I went for healing prayer ministry, the first thing that one of the facilitators said to me prophetically was, "You need to forgive your mother for abandonment". I hadn't said anything to her about the fact that I had been placed in a children's home when I was two years old. As soon as the director said that to me, I knew that she was referring to that event even though I had no conscious memory of that time. I wasn't even aware that I had judged my mother in relation to this, but when I heard this, it rang true.

It took a prophetic word to show me that I had made a judgement against my mother at two years old. From that time, I had carried the lie that I had been abandoned by my parents. Only the Holy Spirit can expose the hidden things within us and give us the keys to breakthrough and healing.

CHAPTER EIGHT

Parental Influence

If our parents were born again, chances are we would have much better foundations than those who are still in darkness. However, there are many dysfunctional Christian families with parents that, because of their own prior poor foundations are still in the process of restoration, and there are also non-Christian families who have had better foundations than some Christians and are able to provide reasonably good, stable environments for their children. Whatever the case may be, God has a destiny for each of us and He wants us to prosper and be blessed and to restore us.

It is so important that we discipline our children with love and not place unrealistic expectations upon them. Ephesians 6:4 says, *"Fathers, do not provoke your children to anger, but bring them up in the discipline and instruction of the Lord"* while Colossians 3:21 (NIV) echoes this by saying *"Fathers, do not embitter your children, or they will become discouraged".*

Oftentimes, parents can discipline their offspring in a way that imparts shame, and a sense of, "You're not allowed to make mistakes". When this happens, a child may only feel loved when they "perform" correctly or conform to a parent's expectations of them. Harshness in parental discipline can lead to a rebellious spirit taking root within a child's soul. Placing too high an expectation upon children's performance can also make them feel that they're only valuable when they're performing. I thank God that He is not like that.

Many times, while ministering to others I've come across people with a perfectionist/performance spirit because they feel that the only way that they can be loved by God and others is to perform and be perfect, which we know is impossible.

One lady I prayed for years ago began laughing when I prayed over her releasing the perfectionist/performance spirit from her life. She said, "I'm fifty-something years old and I've just realized that I'm allowed to make mistakes". This was very liberating for her.

Some may grow up with parents who attend a church with a 'religious spirit' (more about this later) and this legalistic spirit can also make them feel that they need to perform to be loved by God and others. When this is the case, we need to break the negative soul ties with this spirit and those people who taught us that. We must renounce and repent of our agreement with the lie that we can't be loved if we're not perfect. We then need to receive the truth that God loves us just as we are at this stage of our journey and that we live within His grace as we grow in Christ. The truth is that it is only when we are in a safe place of feeling loved and valued by God that we are enabled to make a recovery and be transformed. Acceptance and love set a solid foundation for us from which we can gain recovery.

Parental blessing

The Father's blessing was of great significance in Old Testament times. Parental blessings are still relevant today. I've seen Christian parents withhold their blessing from their offspring's marriages if they don't approve of their choice of partner and even boycott their wedding. This attitude only causes a rift in relationships and if their son or daughter's choice is not the best, they will need all the support that they can get.

Sometimes it is good to have a mature Christian male or female to stand in proxy as parents for us as a mother and/or father to pronounce a parental blessing when this has been lacking in our lives.

Parents create ungodly soul ties with their offspring when they seek to manipulate or maintain control over them once they have reached adulthood. Scripture tells us that children should obey their parents, however as children enter adolescence, parents need to learn to little by little, give them more say in their lives, according to the wisdom and maturity of the individual. However, once our offspring are adults, God's order is that they must now be fully accountable to Him for their decisions and their lives.

Some parents may say, "Well they're not walking with the Lord, or listening to Him". That may be the case, but we step out of God's order by trying to control them and thereby hinder His ability to work in their lives. Nagging adult offspring about anything including the things of God, only serves to put their backs up and to convey the message to them that they are not as acceptable to you as they would be if they were Christians or did things your way. If God shows us unconditional love, then this is how we walk towards our adult children, regardless of their life choices.

Our responsibility as parents of adult offspring is to support them in their decisions and then trust in the power of prayer to guide them regardless of whether we agree with them or not. This does not mean that we must rescue them from any erroneous choices that they make. As adults, we all are responsible for the consequences of our own choices that we make in life, and rescuing others does not enable them to learn valuable life lessons.

We step into God's shoes when we try to play 'Holy Ghost Junior' in the lives of others. We also need to be aware that we are not to use prayer in a way to manipulate others to align them to **our** will. We may think the person that our offspring is dating is not a suitable spouse for them, but God sees the end from the beginning. As we're not always certain of God's will, we can say, "Lord, I'm concerned about this situation, and I pray that your guidance and direction will be upon them and that your will and purpose will be done in this". If we feel that a sport or hobby is potentially danger-ous, we can ask God to protect them and again, give them wisdom and direction about that issue but we don't tell God to stop them from doing it or how to do it.

If we do this, we are using prayer as a power outside of our-selves, to control others and that control is the sin of witchcraft. As we touched on earlier, whatever spirit we come into agreement with will control that area of our lives and affect those around us. We give the enemy access to our souls as well as others around us by trying to manipulate and control them through actions or prayer. Sometimes this controlling spirit gains access to a person's life through fear. If you have issues with this, you will need to deal with the fear or potential trauma that is driving the behavior and repent of and break soul ties with the spirit of control.

I have seen parents manipulate their children and others to get their own needs met, which is a form of idolatrous, false dependency, as God has already promised to supply all our needs according to His riches in glory (Phil. 4:19). In doing this they are relying on others to fulfill them or provide for them instead of God.

Parents who were not well nurtured in their own childhood or who have arrested development through childhood trauma, can sometimes "invert" their relationship with their children and manipulate them to try to get their children to nurture 'them'. This sort of behavior will psychologically damage our offspring and damage their capacity for future relationships. Many people who have had this kind of parenting can develop an overactive sense of responsibility towards others.

If we belong to God, then we should look to Him as our source of provision and allow Him to heal our insecurities and fears that create dysfunction. We all need support, but we should not unduly depend upon others, especially not our children, to fulfill and support us. Sometimes parents who do not function well socially can be overly emotionally and socially dependent upon their children for their relational needs and have trouble releasing them into adulthood. They live a very 'insular' lifestyle which can hinder their children's ability to socially interact well in the future. If we are to function well in society, we should have a network of friends and family so that we can be balanced. If we belong to a church fellowship, we should be able to enjoy friendship with many people of differing ages.

Our children are not an extension of ourselves. Parents should assume no more right to control their offspring once they become adults than they would seek to control someone outside of their own family. If we do this, we are relegating them back to the status of a child. This imbalance is sure to bring resentment and damage relationships, while also creating spiritual blockages for all involved. If asked for your opinion from your adult offspring, share it in humility. If your opinion differs from theirs then humbly explain why you think differently. However, if they don't agree with you in the long run, bless them anyway and keep praying God's direction over them, not your will. Allow them the same freedom of choice that God allows you.

We should never seek to plan a child's destiny for them. For instance, in the case of a family business where parents might automatically assume that their son or daughter should take on the responsibility for running it later in life. That business might have been your life's ambition, but it may not be your offspring's desire, gifting, or calling. God may have another plan for them.

If, as a parent you have done this, then you will need to repent and ask God to forgive you and heal your soul in this area. Then cut the ungodly soul ties between yourself and your children and break off any spirit of control attached to them. Apologise to your children for this and let them know that you will support and respect their rights to make their own decisions in the future.

If you are the adult offspring of a parent who is doing this, bind the spirit of control behind it, forgive them, and break the ungodly soul ties with them also. This does not mean that you are cutting all soul ties from that person, but only the unhealthy ones. If you can, speak with your parents about this and let them know that this is not profitable.

Deficits in parenting skills

I heard a family psychologist once say that a lot of women who have had repeated childhood trauma often will cope well enough in life until they have children of their own. When we haven't been nurtured well and have lacked personal support, we can have an empty emotional tank, so when others want to draw from our internal resources, we can feel stressed because we have very diminished emotional reserves. This doesn't mean that we don't love our children and want the best for them, but simply that we have limited resources with which to do it.

Internal retreat

Lack of personal bonding with parents and past unresolved trauma can lead to being emotionally disconnected from others and life. This type of background can leave us lacking in a sense of relevance or significance. Many people like this tend to live in an isolated world inside themselves. Trauma can cause people to implode within themselves. Just as a demolition team will set up explosive charges inside a building to cause it to implode within itself rather than explode outwardly, people can implode internally.

They may feel that the world is not a safe or friendly place to live in and that there is no one that they can trust.

For those who experience this internal collapse, some can build up fantasy worlds that are much more appealing to them than reality and this provides a sense of emotional fulfillment that is lacking in their daily lives. In that unreal world, they can be the most attractive, accomplished, valued person that their hearts desire to be and everything that they feel that they fail to be. They can become addicted to the fantasy of novels, electronic games, or television shows because again, their own daily life does not fulfill them due to their damaged emotions and social disconnection. After all, if no one else nurtures you, naturally a person will overcompensate by seeking to nurture oneself which can become obsessive. Other forms of self-nurture may be indulging excessively in interests, hobbies, gambling, drinking, drugs, eating excessively, or sexual sin. Some may even have unhealthy, excessive religious practices. Some of these things are not necessarily sinful or bad in themselves, but it becomes unhealthy when we falsely depend upon something outside of God for our fulfillment, hence it gets out of balance.

You can see why it is very confronting when people who have withdrawn from reality have children. When parenthood deprives them of much of their personal comfort and basic needs such as sleep and personal time, this then drags them back into the cold, hard reality of life. A lack of practical support from a spouse or extended family can leave one feeling alone, under pressure, and without help. This can exacerbate anxiety and fear which undermines one's ability to cope.

When we have been traumatized and/or neglected in our foundational years, we become fearful about not having our needs met. Trauma itself locks us into the stronghold cycle of numerous unhealthy thoughts and behavioral patterns. Unless trauma is released first in deliverance, we cannot have all the emotions and memories associated with those past traumatic events healed. It also makes it hard to forgive those who have that have caused the trauma.

After coming to Christ, God becomes our Father, Nurturer, and Provider, and our concept needs to shift from self-nurture or manipulating others to nurture us, to dependence upon our Heavenly Father. It can take time to break stronghold thinking and emotional patterns of self-protection and self-nurture and to come into a place of rest and dependence upon our Heavenly Father who knows all our needs and who looks after us.

When we have lacked nurture or experienced trauma in our relationship with our parents our perception of a Heavenly Father can be distorted because that concept is being "filtered" through damaged emotions and thought processes related to our own personal experience of a father and/or mother. We need to have every soul wound relating to our parents healed so that we can relate to Father God in a healthy way.

We also must break the stronghold images of our negative childhood experiences of a father/mother through the Name of Christ and the power of the Spirit and then renounce the lies that we have believed about Father God. This may be as simple as praying, "Father, I repent of believing the lie that You are anything like my earthly father/mother" or perhaps "I repent of believing that you are as indifferent to me as my earthly father/mother was". Whatever we have emotionally taken on board in our concept of a parent that does not align with the goodness of the Father that Christ represented to us, needs to be renounced and replaced with truth and we will need to have our hearts healed from wounds and deficits left by our natural parents.

Emotional poverty impairs an individual's self-esteem and worth, so they can become highly sensitive to and even expectant of criticism and judgement from others. Having a good integral sense of self-esteem is a bit like having an emotional cushion inside us that protects us from the buffering that we can receive from circumstances and others in life, and it also helps us bounce back. When this is absent, criticism from others hits a wellspring of feeling bad about oneself. This then reinforces that sense of disapproval and rejection a person may have felt from childhood years and exacerbates anger as well.

This is why we must find the childhood roots of negative emotional responses and behavior otherwise when we try to deal with a current issue, it's like pulling off the top of a weed and leaving the root system behind. Until past rejection, criticism, disappointment, anger, etc. are dealt with and forgiven, we will still respond to other people and situations out of our wounded souls.

We must always replace lies with truth. For instance, if we feel unloved, we must go to the word of God and meditate upon scriptures such as John 15:9. (NIV) *"As the Father has loved me, so have I loved you. Now remain in my love"*.

Ephesians 2:4-5 (NIV) *"But because of his great love for us, God, who is rich in mercy, 5 made us alive with Christ even when we were dead in transgressions—it is by grace you have been saved."*

I knew a man from church years ago who lacked parental love because he was brought up in an orphanage. He was probably around sixty at the time that I was acquainted with him and yet even though he had been a Christian for a long time, he still had an orphan mentality. He always struggled with issues of self-esteem, and connecting with God and he failed to maintain consistent financial stability and employment. God wants us to prosper in every area of our lives, but you can see from this, how strongholds within our souls hinder the development and blessings that God wants to give us in our lives. We need spiritual discernment to identify where the enemy is keeping us captive.

Recently, I ministered to a lady who had been married for many years to a narcissistic man who was repeatedly unfaithful to her. He would leave her and then come back again when it suited him, and she would constantly allow him to abuse and diminish her. He was very controlling, and she always tried to comply with him in whatever he wished her to do. After many years she finally left him, yet she found that he would keep on trying to find ways of access to her. This is very common with that type of personality. They don't want you, but they don't want to let go of you either. They like to feel that they still have some control over you.

The initial time that I ministered to her I asked her why she had allowed him to mistreat and abuse her for so many years and she just looked at me like she didn't understand what I meant. She had become a Christian after she had married, and she said that she felt that she had to forgive him every time that he was unfaithful to her. During our next ministry session, I felt to ask her if there had been other controlling people in her life, and instantly said, "Oh yes, my mother was very controlling".

After ascertaining this we were able to see where she had become conditioned to being so compliant in the face of this type of control. She had a great deal of trouble trusting her own opinion to the point that she found it hard to make the most basic decisions like, 'should I buy this, do I really need it or what will I do with my day'? She was constantly 'second guessing' herself. I encouraged her that she had a God-given right to make personal choices that did not really need to be viewed as right or wrong. It will take time for her to recover her freedom of choice and identity, but with continued ministry and breaking soul ties to those controlling spirits she is on her way to recovery.

Illegitimacy in the family bloodline

If you were born illegitimately or it is in your bloodline, often-times you will feel that you are not as significant or relevant as other people. Satan will take every opportunity to oppress us, especially when peoples' origins and conceptions have come out of the covering and alignment of God's divine order. The following information shows how rejection, abandonment, hiding, insecurity, and shame come upon children born illegitimately.

> *"Satan will use any opening he can to bring torment against the children of God. Illegitimacy and incest are the only two curses in the Bible that affect ten generations. A person of illegitimate birth shall not enter the assembly of the Lord; none of his descendants, even to the tenth generation (Deut. 23:2 AMP). From the inception of this curse, ten generations equals 2048 descendants!*
>
> *The latest statistics published by the Center for Disease Control show that 40.6% of all births are born to unmarried parents. The number is astounding. Last year that number was 1,595,873 children.*

> *"Many clients know their parents considered aborting them. This knowledge immediately invites demonic spirits of rejection and insecurity to begin their destructive work. I remember when I first started noticing a pattern of these five tormentors with a client years back. She always felt disconnected. She called herself the "black sheep" of the family. She isolated herself and hid in fear as a child. This pattern continued into adulthood as she hid to avoid family gatherings. She had trouble staying connected to the Church.*

> *Her devotional time was hindered. She told me that she had trouble reading the Bible and entering into worship. When I was praying for her, I saw her mother wearing an overcoat. I asked her, "Did your mom hide her pregnancy from her parents in shame?" She told me that her mother was able to conceal her pregnancy until she was almost due. The root of torment was her illegitimate conception. Her deliverance was profound".* **https://aandbcounseling.com/5-demonic-spirits-torment-illegitimate-children/**

Many people can have an orphan spirit even if they've had parents. If there has been a lack of parental validation, interaction, and support in their lives, they can carry that stronghold identity even after being born-again.

> Romans 8:15 (NIV) *"The Spirit you received does not make you slaves, so that you live in fear again; rather, the Spirit you received brought about your adoption to sonship. And by him we cry, "Abba, Father."*

CHAPTER NINE

Importance of Priorities In Building Healthy Family Foundations

Often as Christians, we think of overt "sin" as being the cause of all our troubles. We all know about the destructive power of sin, but family dysfunction can be just as destructive as sin in a person's life and in the way that this impacts those around them.

One woman I knew in a church many years ago was the daughter of Christian parents who had failed to nurture her well in her formative years. Both of her parents had experienced childhood trauma and dysfunctional family backgrounds and still had many issues to overcome themselves. The father was a workaholic who did not take time to nurture his wife and children. He was an aloof man who disciplined in a harsh manner. The mother was very emotionally dependent upon her children. She had inverted her relationship with the eldest daughter and wanted the daughter to nurture her and take over some of her home-life responsibilities for her. Subsequently, due to emotional deficit and other factors, the daughter developed an eating disorder during her early teen years and struggled with successive unsuccessful, broken relationships for many years after. The many broken relationships consequently impacted her and her children in an extremely negative way, leading one of the children to take her own life. Sadly, this woman never married again.

The point I wish to make is that there was no overt sin in that family's life. They went to church regularly and there were no ungodly practices in their family, but because of unhealed wounds, relational dysfunction, and imbalance of priorities, the enemy was able to gain access to future generations to bring destruction and even premature death.

The sad thing about this type of scenario is that often Christians will say things like, "We don't know why the Lord allowed this or that to happen." But the truth is that the enemy can gain access to Christian families and their offspring through generational sin and dysfunction that had not been dealt with.

God is all about the heart of man, love, and relationship. Without proper love, nurture, validation, and relational connections, whether we grow up in a Christian home being taught Christian principles or not, a person's soul will not prosper, and neither will their relationships.

When we have deep emotional deficits, oftentimes we will look to the next human relationship to fulfill us, and we can easily take our eyes from God as being our primary source of love, provision, and personal care. Many times, I've seen Christian people who are so desperate to fill the emotional void in their souls that they have become vulnerable to accepting the wrong people into their lives.

We can neglect to be prayerful in these matters and may align ourselves with whoever may appear to have affection for us without taking the time to really test their character.

Maintaining balance to avoid dysfunction

An important part of maintaining balance within our lives is to prayerfully examine that which needs to be prioritised in each specific season of our lives. For instance, when we are raising young children, we will have different priorities than when we have elderly parents who may need extra care.

Husbands who do not emotionally nurture their wives and are not hands-on with their children leave an emotional deficit which later may be filled with something unproductive, and these issues can reverberate throughout future generations. People in ministry particularly need to maintain balance with their personal and professional lives. Just because you bring your children up with Christian principles does not mean that they will become healthy, well-balanced adults unless there is proper love and nurture as well. If they have felt neglected in their childhood by their parents because of their parents' ministry, they may feel bitter and resentful of their parents and their parents' 'God' in adulthood.

The average Christian person will make three basic covenants in their lives with God, which consist of their commitment to God at the point of their salvation, their marriage vows before God, and the dedication of their children to God to bring them up in His ways. If we look at these three primary covenants with God, then this is a fairly good indicator of where our true priorities in life lie. Remember Christ promised that if we seek first the kingdom of God and His priorities, He will add unto us all other things (Matt. 6:33).

If we use these covenants as a guide, this will help us to maintain our God-given roles in our personal relationships and with other obligations as well. This will require a very intentional prayer relationship with God. We need to be mindful of prioritizing that which God finds important. God is all about balance. When you look at the delicate balance of the human spirit, body, and soul, or the balance that is required in nature for plant, animal, bird, and marine life to flourish, it makes you realise that life cannot be lived haphazardly. We have all heard that expression, "the tyranny of the urgent". Sometimes we can be driven by what we think is urgent or important, without being led by the Spirit into His priorities for us. It takes a concentrated, prayerful focus in life to reach this place and then maintain it. If God ordains something in our lives, then He will empower us to fulfill it.

One pastor I knew years ago shared with our congregation about his young adult son who had a psychological disorder. The pastor revealed how he had been invited to be a guest speaker at an overseas conference in Singapore with some other Australian pastors. This was quite an honor. But just as he was due to leave for this event, his son had a particularly bad turn. The pastor debated within himself as to what he should do but eventually decided to go and speak at the conference. Sadly, while he was away, his son took his own life. As he was relaying this past event to the congregation years later, he wanted to convey how in hindsight, things that seemed so important to us at the time can blind us to what really matters.

Priorities are so important in life if we are to avoid a dysfunctional lifestyle. Paying hyper-attention to one or two areas of your life while leaving other aspects neglected will always catch up with us eventually. It is like having a field that is divided into many portions and then only cultivating a few of those areas. The places that are left neglected will become overgrown with weeds and become unproductive fallow ground. Another analogy is forgetting to maintain your car because you are too busy going places until it breaks down and needs serious repair. This has happened to many homes and marriages. Scripture tells us that we reap what we sow, but it is also true that we reap that which we do not sow. If we fail to lay the best foundations in our children's lives while they are still young, we cannot get that time back again. I'm not saying that God cannot eventually redeem this situation, but it can create a lot of problems and heartache for all concerned unnecessarily. Prevention is better than cure.

Psychologists use a term called Emotional Object Constancy whereby when a child internalizes the nurture from their parents. This nurture then becomes like an anchor within the child's soul as a sense of security, identity, and well-being. This internal security then enables a person to step out into the world as an independent, confident adult. Well-nurtured people carry within themselves a sense of connection, stability, and support. Without this, people are left feeling anxious, fearful, insecure, and vulnerable to substance abuse.

The following statement is from Willow Springs Recovery, Drug and Alcohol Rehab in Texas:

"Families are related to alcohol abuse and drug addiction in many complex ways, ways we're not entirely sure. Is addiction related to nature or nurture? It looks like both. It looks as if substance abuse can be related to nurturing, or more specifically, a lack of nurturing. We all know that our home environment can shape the way we see the world, how we act and react to it. Why shouldn't things be any different when it comes to alcohol or drug abuse?"
https://www.willowspringsrecovery.com/drug-addiction/ family-nature-nurture-alcohol-abuse-drug-addiction/

Children need the loving guidance of parents especially when they make mistakes. They need to be shown where they have gone wrong, what the potential consequences of their actions could bring and to be taught how to respond in the correct way. Children must always be given boundaries and consequences when it comes to their behavioural development. Discipline, when done in a nurturing way, will bring good fruit in a child's life. It must always be expressed in love and by parents being 'proactive' and not 'reactive' to the situation and always with the child's development and well-being in mind. Scripture tells us to "speak the truth in love".

> Ephesians 4:15 (NIV) 15 *"Instead, speaking the truth in love, we will grow to become in every respect the mature body of him who is the head, that is, Christ".*

This truth also applies to the development of the church. When we are discipled and disciplined in love, we will grow into the mature, fruitful body that God purposed for us to be. We were wired for love. God is love (1 John 4:8) and His design for mankind was that they are valued and nurtured in love. When love is absent in a person's life, it's like a plant that is being deprived of light, water, and nutrients. It may barely survive but will not thrive. Love is so essential to every person.

Here is a passage from a Case Study posted by St. Pauls Collegiate School, Hamilton.

> *"In the United States, 1944, an experiment was conducted on 40 newborn infants to determine whether individuals could thrive alone on basic physiological needs without affection. Twenty newborn infants were housed in a special facility where they had caregivers who would go in to feed them, bathe them and change their diapers, but they would do nothing else. The caregivers had been instructed not to look at or touch the babies more than what was necessary, never communicating with them. All their physical needs were attended to scrupulously and the environment was kept sterile, none of the babies becoming ill.*

The experiment was halted after four months, by which time, at least half of the babies had died at that point. At least two more died even after being rescued and brought into a more natural familial environment. There was no physiological cause for the babies' deaths; they were all physically very healthy. Before each baby died, there was a period where they would stop verbalizing and trying to engage with their caregivers, generally stop moving, nor cry or even change expression; death would follow shortly. The babies who had "given up" before being rescued, died in the same manner, even though they had been removed from the experimental conditions.

The conclusion was that nurturing is actually a very vital need in humans. Whilst this was taking place, in a separate facility, the second group of twenty newborn infants were raised with all their basic physiological needs provided and the addition of affection from the caregivers. This time however, the outcome was as expected, no deaths encountered". **https://stpauls.vxcommunity.com/Issue/Us-Experiment-On-Infants-Withholding-Affection/13213.**

As parents, we can commit ourselves to doing many things that are good, but we must consider how each commitment that we make regarding our time will affect the entire spectrum of our lives. We are responsible for laying healthy foundations in our children's lives and especially in their values and character. We cannot get those years back again if we do not invest wisely in them. It takes healthy boundaries to raise healthy children and we need to teach them how to establish their own boundaries too.

This scenario can be exacerbated if it is combined with parenting that shows little interest in the child's personal desires and opinions, such as allowing them to make some choices for themselves (within reason) or encouraging them to make decisions.

Even just a lack of individual, one on one parental input can make a child feel that they are always in the peripheral vision of their parents and that 'they' and their opinions are not relevant or important. When we become Christians, this concept can also carry over into our relationship with our Heavenly Father and we can feel that we are in His peripheral vision too. We need our souls to be healed and reprogrammed by the Holy Spirit to be able to receive the truth about how God loves and sees us. Scripture tells us that we are the apple of His eye and that God is always watching and caring for us.

> Psalm 121:1-5 (NIV) *"I lift up my eyes to the mountains – where does my help come from? 2 My help comes from the Lord, the Maker of heaven and earth. 3 He will not let your foot slip – he who watches over you will not slumber; 4 indeed, he who watches over Israel will neither slumber nor sleep. 5 The Lord watches over you – the Lord is your shade at your right hand;"*

Judgement and criticism

Living in a negative, judgmental, and critical environment is very damaging not only for children but for all involved. When we are regularly the target of criticism, this damages self-esteem and confidence. We grow up always expecting everyone to see us in a negative light and therefore we also tend to see others in a negative way. When we are frequently shown our faults in anger or disapproval by a parental figure or older siblings, this wounds our soul, and we become very susceptible to shame. This will always impede personal growth and development. It's a bit like taking a pair of pruning shears to a tree that is not producing well and chopping at it relentlessly every time it begins to sprout until it's out of shape and hacked to pieces. Children living in this environment become angry and resentful and very sensitive to criticism in later life.

> Ephesians 6:4 (AMPC) *"Fathers, do not irritate and provoke your children to anger [do not exasperate them to resentment], but rear them [tenderly] in the training and discipline and the counsel and admonition of the Lord".*

This scenario can also lead to a perfectionist spirit where a person may constantly strive for validation and people's approval. If this is the case, we will carry this mindset over into our Christian walk as we can begin to strive for the love and approval of God the Father, when in fact, we already have this. It is when we abide in His love and He abides in us that we produce fruit, (John 15:4) not when we strive and perform.

Because of childhood deficits, even after we become Christians, we can struggle to give love and grace to others, because it was never given to us. Our own reservoir of love and self-worth can be completely desolate and empty. Until we can renounce the lies that we have believed about God, ourselves, and others and have deliverance from the emotional and mental strongholds that we carry, our wellspring will be blocked and hindered from receiving God's love and releasing it to others.

CHAPTER TEN

Discernment

Before we pray for ourselves or others when seeking whole-ness, it is a good practice to ask the Holy Spirit to anoint us for prayer and to reveal to us whatever it is that He wants to deal with at the time. We must never use principles or methods alone to apply to our own or other people's issues. We need to have revelation from the Spirit for the specific keys we need to use in each unique situation to bring breakthrough.

> Jeremiah 33:3 (KJV) *"Call unto me, and I will answer thee, and shew thee great and mighty things, which thou know-est not".*

Sometimes when we ask the Holy Spirit what issue to pray for, He will remind you of a memory from a traumatic event that has already been prayed into. A friend of mine asked for prayer when she felt that she needed to confront someone who had taken advantage of her in a certain situation. Confronting others was something that she found extremely hard to do. Unfortunately, when she approached this person about it, it all blew up in her face and the person had a huge 'meltdown' and claimed that she was being 'falsely accused'. Naturally, my friend was terribly upset about how all this had panned out and she felt that she needed some prayer support.

As we waited upon the Lord, He led her to the memory of a particular incident that had happened to her in her childhood. When she was four years old her brother and his friend had done something wrong to her that distressed her. This seemed so unrelated to what she was currently dealing with, and she had already had prayer ministry relating to that past event, however, this was the memory that God had brought back to her.

We talked about it for a while and at one point I asked her if her parents knew about what had happened to her at the time. She said that eventually, she had told them, so I asked her how they had responded to that. Her reply was, "Oh, all hell broke loose". I then felt by the Spirit that, though the initial incident had been dealt with, there was an area of trauma that was unresolved from that memory which involved the emotional fallout after speaking up for herself.

There was a stronghold where she felt that if she confronted someone, "all hell would break loose" again. The enemy still had an access point because of a wound in her soul that had been left unresolved from this event. This was hindering her ability to voice concerns with other people and to find a resolution. This was a 'tentacle' left behind from that original event that still needed emotional healing.

We always need the Holy Spirit to show us anywhere we have any unresolved traumatic memories. As He reveals things to us, we must command the spirit of trauma and if applicable, violation, to be broken off all the cellular memories that are contained within the neurological pathways of the body in Christ's name. We must also minister healing to anywhere that trauma has affected our nervous system or where the chemical secretions of the body came out of balance in relation to that event. In doing this, we are dealing with the physiological as well as the psychological effects of that trauma. This could be fear, shame, intimidation, anger, or even confusion.

Trauma can bring confusion within a person's soul that can later manifest itself within the body in the form of an auto-immune disorder.

> *"Childhood traumatic stress increased the likelihood of hospitalization with a diagnosed autoimmune disease, decades into adulthood. These findings are consistent with recent biological studies on the impact of early life stress on subsequent inflammatory responses".* **https://www.ncbi. nlm.nih.gov/pmc/articles/PMC3318917/**

Once we have dealt with all the negative effects of trauma, we will need the discernment of the Spirit to locate any lies that we have taken on board through traumatic events. These can be numerous and may include such things as a belief that "all men are untrustworthy", or "we deserved the way that we were treated" etc. Any lies must be revealed to us by the Holy Spirit's divine leading and revelation.

We may also need to ask Him to restore to us a healthy sense of identity, safety, dignity, worth, truth, and purity.

We will need to have the boundaries that were violated and broken, correctly reinstated by the power of the Holy Spirit. Again, we must repent of any ungodly attitudes that we took on board at that time toward God or others. We can then ask the Holy Spirit to initialize and reactivate back into the correct function, any areas where any development was arrested. We may have to persist in prayer until we see a complete recovery.

For those who have repeated abuse and trauma throughout their lifetime, they will require repeated ministry which can take commitment and time. We must be committed to our own recovery and pursue wholeness diligently.

Some of these things can be so ingrained within our soul, that we need times of soaking in the presence of God to allow the Holy Spirit to rise from our regenerated spirit into our soul realm to bring healing and transformation.

All healing and transformation are outworked by the Spirit of God, so anywhere that we are out of balance can be brought under the restoring, resurrection power of the Holy Spirit. Remember at the beginning of the book of Genesis, the Earth was without form and void, but the Spirit of God was hovering, brooding, or incubating over the chaotic mass. When God spoke, the Holy Spirit moved and brought forth the creation of life and order at His word. Our soul realm can be a chaotic, broken, and confused mess of emotional insecurities, hurts, pain, fear, twisted identity, and sinful responses. It takes the divine power of the Spirit of God released into our inner confusion and chaos to remove the blockages and obstacles that hinder us, and to create order and bring restoration to our souls.

God promises to fill the empty, barren places that we all have in varying degrees.

Psalm 107:8-9 (NIV) *"Let them give thanks to the Lord for his unfailing love and his wonderful deeds for mankind, 9 for he satisfies the thirsty and fills the hungry with good things".*

Isaiah 44:3 (NIV) *"For I will pour water on the thirsty land, and streams on the dry ground; I will pour out my Spirit on your offspring, and my blessing on your descendants".*

To recap what we have learned so far when we come to Christ, He awakens our spirit that was dead in sin and trespasses (Col.

2:13) by the power of His Holy Spirit. He then begins working by His resurrection power to transform our soul realm and to cause us to overcome the internal struggles of the soul with which we all battle. However, there are some things that must be dispossessed from our soul before the fruits of the Spirit are manifested through us, just as the Israelites had to dispossess the giants to come into their fruitful Promised Land. We need the discernment of the Spirit and revelatory keys to identify and break strongholds, heal wounds, and initialize and activate areas that have been dormant in our souls.

Some might find it difficult to discern the hidden issues of their own soul, which is why we need to connect with people who have specific gifts in the healing and deliverance ministry to help us facilitate our recovery. We do not always recognize our own dysfunctional issues because they are so familiar to us, that they seem 'normal' or justifiable to us. We need assistance from people who operate in this type of discernment.

James 5:16 (NIV) *"Therefore confess your sins to each other and pray for each other so that you may be healed. The prayer of a righteous person is powerful and effective".*

A while back I went to a podiatrist and normally, they will do a procedure for me where they take some hardened tissue from between two toes and then it will be fine again. But recently, after I'd had the procedure done, I didn't experience the same relief that I would normally have after treatment, so I went back to see them again and the podiatrist said to me, "there's actually a deeper core there that we need to get down to". After that experience, the Lord began showing me an area where there was a deeper wound in an area of my soul that I had already had some ministry for, but it had not yet been fully resolved, and He wanted to heal it.

Boundaries

It is especially important to have healthy boundaries so that we know when to say "no". When a person has had their boundaries violated repeatedly in their childhood years, they will struggle to feel that they have the right to say no or to impose boundaries in situations or with people who are demanding or intrusive.

A gentle, quieter person may find it extremely hard or even impossible to set boundaries about themselves and can often feel taken advantage of by others. They may accumulate anger over a period when they feel that they have been overborn by people with a stronger personality. Many still carry a victim mentality and find it hard to assert their rights.

Conversely, sometimes people's defenses are overactive to protect themselves and they can come across as aggressive. Their response can be that "they" will be the dominant one to avoid being the victim. It will depend upon the personality type as to which way they will handle this.

This is another area where the Lord wants to bring freedom and breakthroughs to those who have been crushed and bruised and are brokenhearted. Sometimes He needs to initialize and reactivate a person's ability to set boundaries and to give them a sense of permission to enforce those boundaries. With others, He might need to deactivate those automatic reactions or trigger points in our soul that are highly defensive because of abuse.

Victims of childhood trauma and violation will often have been told by their abuser not to tell anyone about it. As this will generally be an older person or authority figure, a child's voice can be shut down and this inability to voice personal needs can continue throughout a person's lifetime. Many people with a victim mentality can feel that they are not entitled to the same rights as other people and that they should not ask for those things. The enemy will create a stronghold, 'prison' boundaries about their lives by restricting their God-given permissions and rights.

In my early twenties, I had a situation where a person continually violated my boundaries. I had very strong reactions to this situation and had only been a Christian for about five years, so I was not very mature personally or spiritually. I tried and tried to forgive that person but was unable to do so. I was also unable to speak freely to them about it because my voice had been shut down through childhood trauma. It wasn't until years later that the Spirit of God showed me that I had been trying to deal with the current wound of violation at that time when the original place of violation from my childhood years hadn't been healed and dealt with yet. I still had all the pain and anger of the original wounds plus a "victim mentality". Also, I was probably stunted in my emotional development as well, so therefore I was unable to deal with this as a responsible adult. We need the discernment of the Spirit to get to the foundation of where the violation or any wound first came in and bring it to a place of resolution so that our responses in our current situation are free from any wounds from the past.

CHAPTER ELEVEN

Unresolved Wounds Become Accumulative Over Time

Our wounds become accumulative over time. Years ago, a friend of mine experienced the loss of three close people in her life within a period of about four years. She began to find it extremely hard to function, so she went to a counsellor. The counsellor told her that she had experienced grief, upon grief, upon grief. It took time and ministry to process her grief, because of the accumulation of wounds in her soul.

If you have experienced rejection in your childhood that has not been dealt with and then you experience it again later in life, you will not only feel the pain of the current wound but also the residue of the past incidents where this has happened to you. This is why we must go right back to the root of where a particular wound began to find freedom.

If the church understood the need to process every soul wound effectively at the time of it happening, we wouldn't accumulate wounds that affect our emotional and physical health. For instance, if you've been in a car accident, you will have experienced trauma. If a spouse leaves the marriage, the one left behind can have a myriad of soul wounds such as trauma, rejection, abandonment, fear of the future, and possibly a sense of guilt and failure. A situation like this can really damage a person's self-worth and these things need ministry. I am not saying that we deal with these things in 'one fell swoop', but we need to begin to process our issues from the point of the impact. The time it will take to recover will very much depend on whether it was a small offense or a very traumatic event.

We are very vulnerable to the lies of the enemy at a point of deep hurt, disappointment, or trauma. We can also be susceptible to taking on anger, blame, bitterness, or judgement if we are not careful. The enemy will tell us that if we had been a better spouse, this wouldn't have happened. He will seek to tell you that you'll never be successful in a future relationship, etc. We need to uncover any lies that we have believed about ourselves, others, or God when we have been hurt and to renounce those lies and then break their power, in the authority of Jesus' name.

At one time, I worked as a pastoral carer at a local hospital and while there I met a Christian lady who was struggling with her health and emotional issues from her past. She said to me, "I just don't understand why God hasn't protected me from all of this". I was able to share with her how anger, wounds, trauma, and bad attitudes from our past, give the enemy access into our lives and our physical health until we can receive healing and deal with any ungodly attitudes that we might still have in relation to those wounds.

I was privileged to pray for her and to direct her to a place where she could go to begin receiving ongoing ministry. As I left, she squeezed my hand and said to me, "I believe that God sent you to me today". So many people do not understand the impact of wounds left unresolved in our soul realm and how the enemy creates "prisons" around these places.

Years ago, while working as a beauty therapist, I had a client who had worked in a service station for thirty years, and one day she was held up and robbed at gunpoint. At the time of meeting her, she told me that she had only just begun to come out of her home for short periods of time because she experienced panic attacks whenever she went out. For thirty years she had felt completely safe at work and in society, and then in one short, traumatic encounter, all her security to live and move about freely had been shut down.

You would think that if you had been safe all that time and only one short traumatic incident had occurred, rationally you could surmise that it would be unlikely that this would happen to you again. But trauma is not rational. The heart, the mind, the nervous system, emotions, and memories are all affected by a trauma like this, and this wounding brings brokenness and captivity. This is why Jesus said that He heals the broken heart **and** sets the captive free. The enemy always brings captivity into vulnerable areas of brokenness and in this case the fear was so great that the lady had become captive to a spirit of agoraphobia.

If we have had a history of rejection, for instance, we can develop an expectation of rejection or abandonment that will keep us from allowing others to get close to us. This is also a form of captivity. Oftentimes we can make an inner vow, even as children, that we will never allow someone to get close enough to hurt us again. This expectation and any vows that we make, become a "prison" that keeps us from pursuing healthy relationships with others. It might keep the bad out, but it also keeps the good out as well. Until we deal with these sorts of issues, we hinder God from bringing us to the fullness of all that He has for us.

I had a mature friend in a church a while back who was divorced and single at the time. She had been dating a man in the church for about two years. He had obviously been very wounded by his past marriage breakup and because of this, was unable to commit to a permanent relationship with my friend. Sadly, after some more time passed, she decided to move on because she could see that he was 'stuck' in the past by his wounds and was fearful to make a commitment to her for the future. When we have unresolved issues, this will always hinder us from going forward into the plans and purposes that God has for our lives.

When God filled us with His Spirit at the new birth, His intention was that we would grow to be a channel of His love and healing to others and that we would experience good fruit flowing from our lives.

John 7: 37-39 (NIV) *"On the last and greatest day of the festival, Jesus stood and said in a loud voice, "Let anyone who is thirsty come to me and drink. 38 Whoever believes in me, as Scripture has said, rivers of living water will flow from within them." 39 By this he meant the Spirit, whom those who believed in him were later to receive. Up to that time the Spirit had not been given, since Jesus had not yet been glorified".*

If we have an accumulation of soul wounds, this blocks the living water of the indwelling Spirit from flowing forth.

Never judge another person for their issues. You do not know what has been laid in their foundations and what their personal battle is about. Many people in the church desperately need healing in their soul realm so that they can be all that God has called them to be.

When we go to church, we can receive good teaching, information, and ministry, but unfortunately, few pastors within the Body of Christ are able to first recognize the deeper needs within individuals' lives who have been broken and traumatized, let alone know how to minister to them. Often, we are trying to deal with symptoms rather than the root causes. Most pastors are particularly good

GPs but usually, deeply broken people need "specialists", people with a specific gift of discernment to minister to these types of issues. People can sit in churches year after year carrying painful, unresolved memories. They need deliverance and healing so that they can walk in the freedom and transformation that allows the image of Christ to be formed within them.

Many broken people are very sincere, diligent, earnest Christians, but they can struggle to make progress in certain areas of their lives because of these strongholds. So often they are mis-understood by others in the church. They can be judged as weak Christians, or that they have "not surrendered" their issues and pain to the Lord and this judgement by others continue to add to their hurt and pain. They can also be judged by others because they are always at the prayer ministry line.

Sometimes, they must put up with people, who do not have a clue, trying to "fix" them. Uninvited interference by others only succeeds in making those struggling to feel like everyone sees their faults and evaluates them as "inferior Christians". In fact, their walk is many times harder than the average Christian, and the strength and endurance needed in their journey is far more than anyone can realize.

Counselling, even if it is Christ-based, can support an indi-vidual to some degree while they are receiving prayer ministry as well, but it will not heal the root of the issues because information cannot bring transformation. Psychologists can offer you 'behav-ioral management' techniques but, we don't need to manage our 'stuff,' we need to have our memories healed and to be delivered and transformed through the power of the Spirit of God.

2 Corinthians 3:17 (NIV) *"Now the Lord is the Spirit, and where the Spirit of the Lord is, there is freedom. 18 And we all, who with unveiled faces contemplate the Lord's glory,*

are being transformed into his image with ever-increasing glory, which comes from the Lord, who is the Spirit".

Sometimes, it is not until we are older, and we start to see unhealthy patterns of reactions and attitudes in our lives that we realise the extent of our problems. The Holy Spirit must illuminate these things to us of course, but sometimes He needs evidence to back up what He wants to reveal to us. Our recollection of past experiences allows Him to do this.

Fruit versus works

People who do not grow up with a strong sense of identity and whose gifts and talents have not been discovered in childhood years may become Christians, but instead of finding their identity in Christ, they can live within the confines of their stunted boundaries often doing good works as a way of finding some sort of self-worth and identity. They can become very "Christian" like a label has been stuck on their foreheads, but they have not necessarily found their true self as God intended them to be. Because this form of identity is generated from their own flesh, some can become prideful and competitive with other Christians.

Remember the parable where Jesus talked about the man who gave three men a measure of talents each to invest and how the first man made a large profit and the second, a moderate profit, but the third one was fearful and hid is talents in the ground (Matthew 25:14–30).

Insecurities set boundaries about our lives so that we do not step out and discover or cultivate our natural and spiritual gifts and talents. Because of this, we can fail to go where these gifts could take us into the world to be a light for Him and we are unable to walk in our God-given identity or to fulfill our true purpose in Him. Many people remain within the safe confines of the church and use good works and their "Christian knowledge," to make them feel worthy and purposeful.

Good works do not necessarily equate to good fruit. Sometimes we may help others with the view that we want to be seen as good Christians or because we feel we must earn God's favour. It is our character and the motive of our heart that God is really concerned about.

> 1 Corinthians 3:12-13 (NIV) *"If anyone builds on this foundation using gold, silver, costly stones, wood, hay or straw, 13 their work will be shown for what it is, because the Day will bring it to light. It will be revealed with fire, and the fire will test the quality of each person's work".*

We do not need to perform to feel worthy because we are already made worthy through the sacrifice of Christ. Our greatest fulfillment comes when we find our identity in Christ, and we live purposefully in all that He has predestined for us. There is such great satisfaction in finding our gifts and seeing them bless those around us. To attain this place, we need to identify the fears and stumbling blocks that hinder our progress.

CHAPTER TWELVE

The Nature of Strongholds

When our soul is deeply wounded or traumatized, it is like a fracture within the soul. This becomes a vulnerable place where the enemy will attach himself to those broken places to bring oppression. This is what the Bible refers to as strongholds. They are wounds with demonic attachments. Many people in healing, and deliverance ministries today agree that a Christian can't be possessed, or "filled" with a demon because our born-again spirits are filled with Christ. Therefore, I believe that any demonic attachments are connected to our soul realm, not our born-again spirit, and this is where our true struggle lies. I have heard this described as being like a "Velcro" attachment. The enemy finds areas to 'stick' to our souls and will remain there until we identify it, stop agreeing with it, take authority over it, and remove it in the authority of Christ's name. Then we are positioned to invite the Holy Spirit to come into those areas that were fragmented and heal wounds in our psyche*.

[Greek psychē] –

a: SOUL, PERSONALITY
b: the totality of elements forming the mind

specifically, in Freudian psychoanalytic theory: the id, ego, and superego including both conscious and unconscious components **Merriam-Webster dictionary**.

The enemy and all his torment were defeated at the cross; therefore, it is our responsibility to enforce the power of the cross in the authority in Christ's name and to dispossess 'the giants' or strongholds in our lives that hinder us from possessing our personal promised land.

Ephesians 6:12-13 (KJV) 12 *"For we wrestle not against flesh and blood, but against principalities, against powers, against the rulers of the darkness of this world, against spiritual wickedness in high places"*.

This scripture relates to both our external circumstances and internal battles. Let's look at 2 Corinthians 10:3-5 (KJV) and see what Paul says about this battle of the soul.

"For though we walk in the flesh, we do not war after the flesh. For the weapons of our warfare are not carnal, but they are mighty through God to the pulling down of ***strong holds***. *Casting down every* ***imagination*** *and every high thing that exalts itself against the knowledge of God, bringing every thought captive to the obedience of Christ"*.
(emphasis mine)

In Exodus 15:1 (KJV), after God triumphed over their enemies, Moses and the Israelites sang this song:

"Then sang Moses and the children of Israel this song unto the Lord, and spake, saying, I will sing unto the Lord, for he hath triumphed gloriously: the horse and his rider hath he thrown into the sea".

This scripture can be seen as an analogy of strongholds within our souls, in that the "horse" can represent a wound in our soul that leaves an opening to the enemy, and the "rider" represents the stronghold attachments where the demonic 'sits' upon that wound to keep us bound.

You may have heard the saying that a negative thought left unchecked turns into imagination, and imagination left unchecked can become a stronghold. It is so important to deal with negative imaginations and attitudes when they first present themselves to our minds. When we do not bring a negative thought in submission to Christ, and we dwell upon it for too long, it becomes a stronghold. We need to learn to catch these things at their initial stage.

As adults, we can make decisions to deal with this type of thing effectively if we are aware and informed, but strongholds that were formed in childhood need to be broken. Anger and defensiveness for instance, which is a natural response that tells us that something that someone has done to us is wrong, become a stronghold within a child's soul. Then throughout their lifetime, every new hurt and negative response accumulates until it profoundly affects their well-being.

I spoke to a young man a while back who was not coping well with stress at the time, so he went to see his local doctor. He said to me that the doctor pulled out his desk drawer which was cluttered and said to him, "Imagine that this is your emotional reservoir. At this present time, it is full to overflowing with stress and negative input". Over time accumulative stress can cause "burnout" of the chemical balance of our bodies, and this is where anxiety and depression come in. If this happens, we may need medication to support us during our journey to recovery. This is something that must be decided between you, God, and your physician.

> *"The long-term activation of the stress response system and too much exposure to cortisol and other stress hormones can disrupt almost all the body's processes. This puts you at higher risk of many health problems, including:*
> *Anxiety.*
> *Depression.*
> *Digestive problems.*
> *Headaches.*
> *Muscle tension and pain.*
> *Heart disease, heart attack, high blood pressure, and stroke.*
> *Sleep problems.*
> *Weight gain.*
> *Problems with memory and focus.*
>
> *That's why it's so important to learn healthy ways to cope with your life stressors".* **News Network Mayo Clinic**

When we are angry, God wants us to process that anger before we sleep lest we give the enemy a foothold in our lives (Eph. 4:26). While grace covers our sins in Christ, when we deliberately hold on to something against someone, we give the enemy a legal right to oppress us. God is not angry with us when we are angry, but He wants us to be able to come to Him and allow Him to heal our hearts and enable us to forgive whoever hurt us. This can be a process that takes time, depending on how much unresolved negativity has accumulated within us over the years. We need to remember that while we are working with God towards forgiveness and healing, we are still under His grace.

When children have suffered some form of abuse repeatedly and they have had no power to protect themselves and no ability to remove themselves from their offenders, their ability to trust others is impaired. Oftentimes, it is a parental figure who should have provided security and trust, and who is the one that they fear the most. You can see how people with this sort of background have difficulties with trusting others and can have a lot of residual anger. If their primary caregivers were untrustworthy, then why would they trust anyone else? In later life, they will not be willing to let down their protective boundaries or to be vulnerable to others because intimidation and fear of man have become "set" within their souls. This is a stronghold. In some cases, this repressed anger can lead to aggressive and even violent behavior later in life. Until the hurts and strongholds attached to the foundational root of these reactions are dealt with, a person will not be able to deal with the bad fruit that they are seeking to overcome in their current relationships. This is why just quoting a scripture at a problem like this will not dissolve its effects. This sort of situation requires revelation and deliverance, not just anger management.

Demonic strongholds cause people, as they journey through life, to see things through broken, damaged emotions. It's a bit like wearing dark glasses and perceiving things from a negative point of view.

Because many people's issues relate to the family into which they were born and they still currently have those family connections, they can continue to battle with the effect of these destructive relationships even into adulthood. They may continue to feel judged, criticized, diminished, or attacked by current family members. This then continues to hit the places of their original wounding from which they are trying to recover. There are times when people who are working towards recovery from their past, need to separate themselves or limit contact with destructive relationships, at least for a season, to allow God to heal them. After all, if someone beat you up physically and you were trying to recover from bruises, cuts, and broken bones, would you go back into that person's orbit and allow them to do it again? It is no different regarding emotional abuse. God does not want us to allow others to abuse us. In the meantime, you can pray for those who hurt you and ask God to deliver them from their own issues as you work towards forgiving them and being healed yourself.

General curses and strongholds

Many of our family issues come from generational curses that have been passed on through the ancestral bloodline. We can break these "curses" and negative soul ties to our forebears through the power of Christ's death and resurrection. When addressing this, we need to apply the blood of Christ to our offspring as well. Whatever negative issues that we carry genetically and spiritually that are unresolved within our soul at the time of conceiving our children, can be passed on to them through us and our partner's bloodline. I will give more details regarding this later.

Isaiah 49:24-26 (NIV) "Can plunder be taken from warriors, or captives be rescued from the fierce? 25 But this is what the Lord says: "Yes, captives will be taken from warriors, and plunder retrieved from the fierce; I will contend with those who contend with you, and your children I will save. 26 I will make your oppressors eat their own flesh; they will be drunk on their own blood, as with wine. Then all mankind will know that I, the Lord, am your Savior, your Redeemer, the Mighty One of Jacob."

Trauma and DNA

Trauma from abuse can be perpetuated throughout generations both spiritually and physiologically.

> *"Over the past few years, research has shown evidence of epigenetic inheritance in mice, rats, and even humans. In 2015, a major study from a research team at New York's Mount Sinai Hospital looked at how trauma suffered by Holocaust survivors is capable of being passed on to their children. They analysed the genes of the children of 32 Jewish men and women who had been interned in a Nazi concentration camp during WWII, who experienced tor-ture, or had to hide during the war. They found evidence of genetic changes to one gene associated with the regulation of stress hormones in children that appeared to be related to epigenetic tags on their parents' DNA. This is signifi-cant, because how such genes are regulated can determine how a person deals with stress".* **https://www.gizmodo.com. au/2017/08/can-trauma-experienced-by-your-great-great-grandparents-be-passed-on-to-you/**

Note how trauma tags are identifiable in our DNA and that those genetic markers can be passed on to our offspring. These markers are referred to as epigenetics.

> *"Epigenetics is the study of heritable phenotype changes that do not involve alterations in the DNA sequence. The Greek prefix epi- in epigenetics implies features that are "on top of" or "in addition to" the traditional genetic basis for inheritance".* **https://en.wikipedia.org/wiki/Epigenetics**

It is interesting that the actual sequential code of the DNA is not altered through inherent trauma, but that the genetic aberration actually 'sits on top of' the genetic code like a 'tag' on the DNA. This sounds to me like a demonic stronghold to me.

> *"One of the most interesting and controversial aspects of epigenetics is the concept of inheritance. This suggests that events in our lives can affect our children's development and health, and possibly our grandchildren's. Similarly, experiences our parents and grandparents had before we were born may also impact on our lives.*
>
> *"I think everyone's intrigued by this idea they're part of a history that isn't just about the genes that they have, their DNA, but it's also about the experiences that occurred before them to their ancestors. I think this is such a powerful idea," said Rachel Yehuda, Professor of Neuroscience and Psychiatry at the Mount Sinai School of Medicine, New York.*
>
> *Professor Yehuda studies the impact of traumatic experiences on war veterans, survivors of the Holocaust, of the September 11 attacks, and their children. She's found that children born after the war to Holocaust survivors with post-traumatic stress disorder (PTSD) were more likely to develop PTSD or depression themselves, compared to other Jewish adults.*
>
> *These children also shared epigenetic markers with their parents on a gene that made them more reactive to stress".*
> **https://www.abc.net.au/news/science/2017-04-21/what-does-epigenetics-mean-for-you-and-your-kids/ 8439548#lightbox-share-8449278**

When we have layers of trauma in our souls, our capacity to deal with the stresses of life is significantly diminished. It doesn't take a lot of stress to put us into emotional overload because our wellspring already has a huge reservoir of past stresses and fears. Our defense mechanisms overreact during stressful times, and we will either seek to attack that which appears to be a threat to us or to escape from whatever appears to be the source of the pressure. This is referred to by psychologists as the "Fear, fight, flight response".

> *"The Fight or Flight response is a physiological response triggered when we feel a strong emotion like fear. Fear is the normal emotion to feel in response to a danger or threat.*
> *Fear also has a close relative we call anxiety. The Fight or Flight response evolved to enable us to react with appropriate actions: to run away, to fight, or sometimes freeze to be a less visible target".* **https://www. nottingham.ac.uk/counselling/documents/podacst-fight- or-flight-response.pdf#:~:text=The%20Fight%20or%20 Flight%20response%20is%20a%20physiological,also%20 has%20a%20close%20relative%20we%20call%20anxiety.**

This 'emotional overload' and feeling out of control either can cause people to withdraw from life or conversely, to seek to control situations and/or people about them in an unhealthy way. Sometimes this takes the form of excessive analysing and planning to keep a handle on things and often involves keeping very tight, familiar boundaries about their lives.

Our wounds make us vulnerable to the enemies' strategies and he will try to create ongoing stress that can lead to burnout. We have heard testimonies from many godly people including Sheila Walsh, Joyce Meyer, and Kris Vallotton, of where they went through burnout at some point in their Christian walk because of the residual emotional effects of childhood trauma. This was not because their relationship with God was faulty, nor was it from a lack of scriptural knowledge on their part, but because of unresolved wounds and strongholds. I believe that sometimes God will allow certain things to happen to us to reveal where those unstable foundations from the past are still affecting us today so that He can deal with them and set us free.

Childhood trauma victims can often carry within them a sense of evil foreboding. When a child has lived continually with the expectation of some sort of abuse, this 'sets' within their foundations a continued expectation of evil, which perpetuates itself later in life. This becomes more than a fear. It is a stronghold where the enemy attaches himself to that wounded area of the soul and keeps recycling fearful thoughts and negative expectations. The definition of evil foreboding is as follows: –

(fôr-bō′dĭng) 1. *A sense of impending evil or 2. An evil omen; a portent.* **https://www.thefreedictionary.com/ forebodinglymisfortune.**

Evil foreboding will hinder us from stepping out into unfamiliar places by creating an expectation that something negative may happen to us in an unfamiliar environment, therefore we may limit our lives to what we consider to be 'safe places'. It may attack us when waiting for a doctor's report, or when a family member is late home from work or school. We might need to confront someone regarding an issue and therefore we expect the worst possible outcome. It can also be an expectation of not having your needs supplied emotionally, physically, or financially. Scripture talks about this in Proverbs 15:15 (AMPC),

"All the days of the desponding and afflicted are made evil [by anxious thoughts and forebodings], but he who has a glad heart has a continual feast [regardless of circumstances]".

I once heard it said that regret of the past and fear of the future destroys all our peace of mind and well-being for today. This is so true. Where there are many unresolved strongholds, our minds are held in anticipation of more negative experiences in the future. This however is not the truth of what God says about us, as Jeremiah 29:11 (NIV) says,

"For I know the plans I have for you, declares the LORD, plans to prosper you and not to harm you, plans to give you hope and a future".

To overcome this, it is not just a case of saying you need to renew your mind, however, that is part of overcoming. Firstly, we must break off the spirit of evil foreboding and ask God for discernment as to where this came in and if this needs to be dealt with generationally. If there were doors open to the ungodly spirit realm, we would repent on behalf of our ancestors' sins and our own. We must also renounce any negative lies that we have been believing.

It is vital that the trauma and pain attached to memories are broken off before we seek to receive healing from the memories themselves. Throwing confession of the Word of God at deep-seated trauma and painful memories is like putting a sticking plaster on a heart attack victim. God wants to heal the whole person and to do this He has to first "undo the enemy's stronghold before He heals and restores.

We see many people self-harming and cutting themselves today because of unresolved emotional wounds. Remember the demoniac who was living among the tombs? He ran about naked, crying and cutting himself because he was so tormented by past wounds and demonic spirits. Unresolved wounds and trauma bring torment and keep us attached to the "tombs" from our past. When Jesus healed and delivered the demoniac, scripture tells us that the people of the village came out to find him "saved" (Greek word *sozo*), clothed, and of a sound mind (Luke 8:26).

The word sozo is used 110 times collectively in both the New and Old Testament Scriptures. It is defined as the following: –

"to save, keep safe and sound, to rescue from danger or destruction, from injury or peril

to save a suffering one (from perishing), i.e. one suffering from disease, to make well, heal, restore to health

to preserve one who is in danger of destruction, to save or rescue

to save in the technical biblical sense

to deliver from the penalties of the Messianic judgement

to save from the evils which obstruct the reception of the Messianic deliverance"
https://www.bing.com/?scope=web&mkt=en-AU&-FORM=IE11TR&pc=DCJB

We can see from this word 'sozo' that God's intention is for every person to live in freedom and wholeness in every area of their lives. Christ bore all our sickness and infirmity upon the cross and defeated the enemy and we, as Christians, are in the process of dispossessing the enemy from our lives and taking our promised land.

There are several Christian organisations today that do 'sozo' ministry including some International Healing Rooms. Simply put, Sozo ministry is a series of questions that help to uncover where a person has soul wounds and where the enemy has gained access points to their life. Once revealed, we can then minister to those areas and close any doors that have been left open to the enemy.

GRIEF CAN BECOME A STRONGHOLD

We must always allow the Holy Spirit to minister into our soul realm particularly during any time of grief or mourning. We must submit our sorrow to His comfort and consolation.

Grief – Your Time is Up!
BY PHYLLIS TARBOX

Any emotion that has lingered too long can open a door to demonic oppression. The bible gives clear instruction on a period of time for grieving the loss of a loved one. An unending grieving process is an open invitation for a stronghold of heaviness. Spirits of loneliness, depression, and possibly suicide move in and set up camp. Secular counseling for loss can take years. That's why, as a deliverance minister it's such a blessing to watch the Holy Spirit deliver a person and do the inner healing in minutes.

I had the opportunity to pray deliverance for a woman who had lost her older sister to cancer. Each time her sister's name was mentioned she burst into tears. As we bound the strongman of heaviness and proceeded to cast out loss, grief and loneliness, the Holy Spirit stopped me and showed me the picture the enemy kept flashing in her head when she thought of her sister. It was the deathbed picture of cancer.

At that moment the Holy Spirit gave my prayer partner a picture of what her sister looked like now, dancing in heaven with Jesus. Prior to deliverance she could not get past the first picture. A week after her deliverance she came in beaming. and said, "You know the enemy tried that old picture again, but this time without those spirits driving me from the inside I was able to just say no!" She continued, "I still cry all the time though, except now they are tears of joy." This woman had been able to complete the grieving process for her sister because that spirit of grief was gone from her life.

https://www.bing.com/search?q=grief+your+time+is+ up+by+Phillis+tarbox&qs=n&form=QBRE&sp=-1&gh- c=1&lq=0&pq=grief+your+time+is+up+by+phillis+tar- box&sc=11-39&sk=&cvid=DCA1188C20254147807CBA AEA46B8E93&ghsh=0&ghacc=0&ghpl=

Trigger points

When we have layer upon layer of strongholds and wounds, we are very vulnerable to further hurt. For instance, it is like you might accidentally bump into a person in an area where they have been physically injured, and they may appear to overreact. You may think," I didn't bump it that hard"! But if that place is already extremely sore, it is extremely sensitive. It is the same with our soul. If there is a reservoir of soul wounds, we can have reactions that are "triggered" by the slightest provocation. If we have emotional deficits where our tank of self-worth and validation is empty, when someone criticizes us in some way, we can feel angry and totally diminished.

"When you encounter a trigger after trauma, a strong emotional and behavioral reaction comes over you. It's as if you are reliving that trauma all over again.

The word "triggered" has become a popular term to describe anything that causes emotional discomfort. But for people who have experienced trauma, triggers can be terrifying, all-consuming, and can seemingly come out of nowhere.

Trauma triggers can be anything that reminds you of a past trauma—which might include a certain smell, a particular song or sound, or a piece of clothing. Triggers are unique to the individual". **https://psychcentral.com/health/ trauma-triggers#Sights**

Imagine a child who had severe physical trauma over many years which resulted in many broken bones that had not been attended to. Over the years their bones would set in all sorts of disjointed angles and later in life, their infirmities would be visible for all to see. However, with the soul, we have all these wounds that were 'set' into place both in our formative years and later in life, that need to be reset and realigned. No doctor would attempt to fix all of this in one fell swoop as it would be too traumatic for the patient. God operates on each of us at a pace that we can tolerate even though sometimes we would like to rush our own recovery. He also chooses the order in relation to what wounds He will address at the time.

Protective walls

When we have strongholds like abandonment or rejection, we can make an inner vow that we will never allow anyone to get too close to us or to become dependent upon others because we don't want to be emotionally vulnerable if they were to die or abandon us. This forms blockages in relationships with others and even God, which can make us feel very isolated and alone. We can make inner vows in all sorts of diverse ways, but once we are aware of these ungodly vows we have made, they need to be renounced in Christ's Name. We must break agreement with any ungodly spirit that we have come into alignment with (such as manipulation or control) and then break the effect of these lies from our souls.

Unforgiveness can be a stronghold. Our own overactive sense of self-protection feels the need to 'keep records' of who is unsafe and why we perceive them that way. There can be valid reasons for setting up boundaries at times especially if a person keeps hitting your past wounds through sin or insensitivity.

Because of these unresolved wounds, we can build high defensive walls about ourselves to protect us from being vulnerable. It is rare that a person can allow their "walls" to go down completely all at once. Sometimes, when seeking recovery, we can start with a prayer like, 'I'm willing to be willing to forgive (someone) and let my defenses down before you, please show me Your love and protection in this situation'. It can take time till we come to a place where we feel secure enough in God's love and His control to allow the Holy Spirit to remove defensive boundaries. A significant part of our recovery involves receiving the revelation of the love and protection of God towards us so that we may feel secure enough to let those walls down.

> Song of Songs 2: 8-10 (NIV*) "Listen! My beloved approaches. Look! Here he comes, leaping across the mountains, bounding over the hills. 9 My beloved is like a gazelle or a young stag. Look, he stands **behind our wall**, (emphasis mine) gazing through the windows, peering through the lattice. 10 My beloved calls to me, "Arise, my darling. Come away with me, my beautiful one. . ."*

In these beautiful verses, we see how our Saviour will jump over hills and mountains, which represent the obstacles and protective boundaries in our lives, to call us out into freedom. He peers through our defensive walls and calls to us to trust Him in His love for us and to rise into liberty and relationship with Him. It is only as we have our souls healed that we can fully respond to Him and be open to His call.

Letting our defensive walls down does not mean we have to go back to an abusive relationship. We are only asking God to remove the residual defenses that are blocking our current relationships with Him and others.

Sometimes, in the process of recovery, we can feel over-whelmed and dismayed with everything that we think is "wrong" with us. While it is vital that we pursue wholeness diligently to have the fruit of the Spirit in our lives, we can't afford to make our problems the center of our focus in life. We must keep our eyes on Jesus and prioritise our relationship with Him. We must also keep a balanced approach to our lives, taking time to do things that we enjoy and help others on the way. Our focus should be on Christ and His love, and His saving, and healing power, not on just our personal issues. Having said that, if you know that you have a lot of issues that need healing and choose to 'sweep these things under the rug' then you are not seeking first the kingdom of God because Jesus said that the kingdom is within you. The fruits that God wants to bring to our lives in the present will be stymied if we do not deal with issues from our past. We need to allow God to reveal each step of our recovery to us by His Spirit and allow Him to lead us in our recovery.

We also need to understand that while waiting challenges us, there may be things that we need to learn during that waiting pro-cess. This is an important part of our character development. We need to surrender to and accept God's timing and be willing to keep our hearts submitted to His ways. This is hard at times because waiting always stretches us.

Abraham and Sarah waited twenty-five years, desperately longing for the promised child and this tried their faith. Joseph was in Egypt and imprisoned for about twelve years feeling that his life was wasting away and that he was abandoned and forgotten.

Yet through this time, he allowed God to refashion his character in such a way that, at the appointed time, God was able to promote him to the highest governmental position under the Pharoah in the land of Egypt. Our journey is not just about pursuing and receiving our healing or breakthroughs but also allowing the character and nature of Christ to be formed within us during our suffering.

During a long period of suffering or waiting we can frequently 'hit the wall' with our faith and patience. However, when we choose to pick ourselves up and, by a determination of our wills, choose to trust God and accept His timing, this act brings transformation and growth to our souls. It's a bit like body-building. Rigorous weight-lifting creates small tears in the muscle tissue. To prevent further injury to the muscle, your body's repair job makes the wounded muscle even bigger and more resilient. As good soldiers in His Kingdom, we must allow the processes of God to work and build faith and good character. We also need to remember that this life is not "it". We have received an eternal inheritance where there will be no more troubles or tears. If we can get our heads around that, we can have a more positive perspective on our current trials.

> Romans 8:17-18 NLT *And since we are his children, we are his heirs. In fact, together with Christ we are heirs of God's glory. But if we are to share his glory, we must also share his suffering".*

While we know that God could heal everything all at once, He doesn't always choose to do things that way. When we strive against God and the way that He does things, we are in rebellion. This ungodly response is another 'wall' we can hit in the process of our growth and holiness. Another layer of self and grumbling must die as we choose to surrender to His methods and timing and to believe and trust Him for our recovery.

CHAPTER THIRTEEN

Pride

Pride was the original sin that saw Satan cast out of Heaven. The reason for His downfall was that He wanted to be equal with or 'like God'.

> *"Satan was once a cherub and a part of the divine council[8]. Before his fall, he had great authority[9] among the angels and heavenly creatures. He was the first heavenly creature God created[10]. He was also one of the guardian cherubim, who protected God's throne. He had the most authority being the firstborn. He clearly had many roles to play in heaven".* **https://medium.com/nutsandboltsofbible/ the-biblical-story-of-satan-687bafa6aa6c**

When Satan tempted Eve to eat the forbidden fruit in the Garden of Eden, he told her that if she would eat of that fruit that she would be 'like God'. Most of mankind still wants to be the 'God' of their own lives.

What an amazing contrast to the humility of our Saviour, Jesus Christ.

"Phil. 2:6-7 *"Though he (*Christ*) was God, he did not think of equality with God as something to cling to. Instead, he gave up his divine privileges; he took the humble position of a slave and was born as a human being. When he appeared in human form, he humbled himself in obedience to God and died a criminal's death on a cross"*.

The humility of our God never ceases to astound me. To think that He would love His creation so much that He would leave His throne in glory to identify with mankind and sacrifice Himself by a very painful death for our redemption is astounding!

When I read the account of the Last Supper where Christ removed His robe and washed His disciple's feet, I find it hard to take it in. He could have just instructed His disciples to wash each other's feet, but He displayed humility and servanthood by His own example.

As strange as this may sound, pride can be a stronghold in the life of a person who has extremely low self-esteem. This seems like a contradiction, but it's quite common. We all have a varying measure of pride in our lives and issues with our own self-esteem. Unfortunately, this is part of our human walk, and we will never 'arrive' at a place of permanent humility in this life. Humbling our hearts and surrendering our affections, desires, will and identity to Christ is something that we as Christians must continually practice.

When we have low self-esteem, we don't want other people to know it, so we tend to create a 'public image' that we hold in place to promote ourselves in other people's eyes and to protect ourselves from feeling diminished. In doing this we try to build our self-esteem by means of our own flesh or performance, but Jesus said, *"That which is born of the flesh is flesh; and that which is born of the Spirit is spirit"* (John 3:6 KJV). If we try to rebuild our lack of self-esteem, or any other area of our life, from our own strength or fleshly nature, it will, in fact, corrupt our soul with pride and self-righteousness.

> Galatians 6:8 (NIV) *"Whoever sows to please their flesh, from the flesh will reap destruction; whoever sows to please the Spirit, from the Spirit will reap eternal life".*

When we struggle with a lack of identity and self-worth, we need to humble our hearts before God and bring our issues to Him to have Him heal and transform these deficits. We need to forgive those who failed to build these things into our foundations. We must spend time with Him asking Him to fill our deficits and then dwell upon His word relating to our identity in Christ. In doing this, we are allowing His Spirit to rebuild our foundations in this area. We need him to fill the empty valleys of our inner man. Only He can bring balance and truth into our identity, worth, and character.

When our self-esteem is extremely low, depending upon our current success or performance, we can swing from feeling bad about ourselves to being very prideful. It can be a bit of a see-saw experience. Even as Christians, if we have deep deficits within our souls, we are not always able to connect to others with pure motives. It is difficult to have a heart that wants to represent Jesus when we are so busy trying to find, build, and promote our own self-image. We can be desperately searching for our own sense of identity and worth, but no one can find their real identity outside of a relationship with God. Human beings are intrinsically valuable because we are the creation of God and loved by Him, not because of our performance or status.

In the extreme, the carnal building of one's own self-esteem can become a form of self-idolatry where all our motives are focused on people's validation and approval. I have personally known a couple of Christians who have had narcissistic personality disorder (NPD). When they aren't trying to impress others with superficial things in their lives, they are constantly making themselves out to be more superior Christians than those around them. People with this personality disorder don't just want to be as good as everybody else, they want to be better than everyone else. This is not Christ-like. Because of this, they are not team players with a focus on unity with others in the Body of Christ. This attitude frequently offends others and therefore they don't have many friends. You will often find that they think that they know more than their Pastor and they will fail to stay connected to a church family for any length of time. One man with this problem, in justifying himself in this, actually said to me, "I'm like Jesus, I stand alone". I'm not saying that everyone who has pride is narcissistic because this is a specific personality disorder.

However, when God wants to shine His light on an issue like pride in our lives and we will not acknowledge it, or we seek to justify our dysfunction, we take ourselves into deception. Jesus spoke about this in Matthew 13:14-15 (NIV).

14 "In them is fulfilled the prophecy of Isaiah: 'You will be ever hearing but never understanding; you will be ever seeing but never perceiving. 15 For this people's heart has become calloused; they hardly hear with their ears, and they have closed their eyes (my emphasis). Otherwise, they might see with their eyes, hear with their ears, understand with their hearts and turn, and I would heal them'".

Note in verse 14 God says 'they have closed their eyes'. I once heard someone expound upon this text by saying that when people see the light of God and are reluctant to respond, it is like they 'squint' at the light so that they minimize its impact upon them.

I have noticed over the years that a lot of men in particular, who have been emotionally wounded and have very low self-esteem, can't even bear to acknowledge their faults to others even to find recovery. Because of this, they get caught in a cycle of denial and self-justification. By doing this, they remain in their destructive behavioral patterns which destroys their relationships with others and church connections too.

Many times, shame is a big part of this reluctance to 'see the light'. This is an area that needs to be discerned by the Spirit of God. When we have complex issues, we need ministry from others to get to the roots of where that sense of shame first came into that person's life. No one should feel that everybody needs to know their personal issues, but we all need at least one trustworthy mentor or place that we can go to when we need help with whatever we struggle with in life.

Our problems need to be shared only with reliable, mature people who are gifted in this area of healing and who will remain discreet about any information shared with them. We need to be fully aware that there is no condemnation to those who are in Christ Jesus (Romans 8:1) while we are working on our personal issues. God knows our past and knows all about our problems when we come to Him. His love towards broken, difficult people is unconditional but unfortunately, this is not always the case with Christian people. So, if you have a lot of unresolved soul wounds, hanging around with people who are equally wounded or who act superior to you may not be the best choice while you are trying to recover. If you're in a season of recovery don't choose to keep company with people who keep on adding hurt to your issues that are not healed yet. Make sure that you have healthy supportive relationships surrounding you. Whatever you do, don't isolate yourself from others when you are struggling.

The wonderful thing in the body of Christ is that we can find 'surrogate' mothers and fathers in the faith to help us along our journey in life. It's important to be aware that if we have problems with trusting people and we do find someone who is dependable, that we must not "fixate" upon this person and expect them to be

113

our "all in all". In doing this we are making them an idol. They are not our saviour nor are they perfect human beings, so we need to be careful that we do not become overly dependent upon a particular individual for help, or place expectations upon them that they can't meet. Our primary focus must always be on Christ as our Saviour and provider.

Self-Idolatry is a stronghold

An important part of recovery involves acknowledging and repenting of any idols that we have falsely depended upon as well as self-idolatry. We must also lay down and surrender any false images and pedestals that we have erected for ourselves within our own imaginations (or souls) and allow God to put this to death within us. This includes any false Christian personas that we have presented to others as well. We need the consistent ministry of the Holy Spirit to rebuild the broken foundations of our personality and identity. Dismantling idolatrous patterns of behavior does not happen overnight but God will deal with these issues in His timing.

CHAPTER FOURTEEN

Negativity and Negative Soul Ties – Roadblocks to Healing

Negativity and complaining

The enemy can frequently gain access into our lives if we practice grumbling and complaining. If you have had a negative history of brokenness, it is very difficult to have a happy expectation of the future. As mentioned before, childhood neglect and trauma hardwire a child's brain to have a future expectation of living in a harsh or even hostile environment. It is quite common for broken people to be negative and develop a habit of grumbling and complaining.

Let's look at an instance in the Old Testament where God's people started to complain during a challenging time. They had been delivered out of Egypt and were travelling through the wilderness while on their way to the Promised Land. God had given them a cloud by day to protect them from the sun and a pillar of fire at night to keep them warm. He had provided manna for them to eat each day and gave them water by supernatural means when they were thirsty, yet they only saw the negative. They still had a negative, poverty mentality from being captive as slaves for many generations in Egypt.

> Numbers 21:4-6 (NIV) *"They traveled from Mount Hor along the route to the Red Sea, to go around Edom. But the people grew impatient on the way; 5 they spoke against God and against Moses, and said, "Why have you brought us up out of Egypt to die in the desert? There is no bread! There is no water! And we detest this miserable food!" 6 Then the LORD sent venomous snakes among them; they bit the people and many Israelites died".*

Today, we are under God's covenant of grace in the New Testament, so God does not 'send' the enemy to punish us because Christ took our punishment for us, however, as we saw earlier about the power of agreement if we choose to agree with God, this will release blessings, but if we choose to agree with the enemy and grumble, **we** give him right of access into our lives. I once heard someone say, "grumbling is the worship language of the devil". Our choices are important. This is why we must develop an attitude of gratitude and maintain a spirit of praise and thanksgiving along life's journey. Many times, we will have to go against our personal feelings and praise God deliberately. This is what is called a 'sacrifice of praise' (Hebrews 13:15). We cannot afford to give the enemy further access to our souls when we are going through trials so we must make sure that we control our tongues. Instead of reacting to circumstances, we must deliberately say what God's word says about our lives and who we are.

Renewing our mind and controlling our tongue is a process that takes time, but the Holy Spirit is with you to help you catch those thoughts, to put them off as He restructures our mental and emotional processes.

Negative soul ties

The enemy can also gain access to our lives through ungodly soul ties. Often, when we have lacked affection, we can be vulnerable to creating ungodly soul ties with people who may not be a good influence over us. Many soul ties are healthy, but we need to identify those that are not.

"The Bible speaks of what is today known as soul ties. In the Bible, it doesn't use the word soul tie, but it speaks of them when it talks about souls being knit together, becoming one flesh, etc. A soul tie can serve many functions, but in its' simplest form, it ties two souls together in the spiritual realm. Soul ties between married couples draw them together like magnets, while soul ties between fornicators can draw a beaten and abused woman to the man whom in the natural realm she would hate and run from, but instead she runs to him even though he doesn't love her, and treats her like dirt. In the demonic world, unholy soul ties can serve as bridges between two people to pass demonic garbage through. I helped a young man not too long ago break free from downright awful visitations from demons, all due to an ungodly soul tie he had with a witch. The man was a Christian, and the only thing that allowed her to send demonic torment his way is through the soul tie. Other soul ties can do things such as allow one person to manipulate and control another person, and the other person is unaware to what is going on or knows what is going on, but for no real reason, allows it to continue.

I believe there are other ways in which soul ties are formed, but here are some that I am aware of.

Sexual relations: Godly soul ties are formed when a couple are married (Ephesians 5:31, "For this cause shall a man leave his father and mother, and shall be joined unto his wife, and they two shall be one flesh."), and the Godly soul tie between a husband and the wife that God intended him to have is unbreakable by man (Mark 10:7-9). However, when a person has ungodly sexual relations with another person, an ungodly soul tie is then formed (1 Corinthians 6:16, "What? know ye not that he which is joined to an harlot is one body? for two, saith he, shall be one flesh."). This soul tie fragments the soul, and is destructive. People who have many past relationships find it very difficult to 'bond' or be joined to anybody, because their soul is fragmented.

Close relationships: King David and Jonathan had a good soul tie as a result of a good friendship (1 Samuel 18:1, "And it came to pass, when he had made an end of speaking unto Saul, that the soul of Jonathan was knit with the soul of David, and Jonathan loved him as his own soul."), but bad soul ties can form from bad relationships as well. Idolizing somebody can cause a bad soul tie.

I have heard too that you can create a soul tie with a rock group by becoming obsessed with their music. This explains the strong pull towards certain music that seems almost irresistible.

Vows, commitments, and agreements: Vows are known to bind the soul (Numbers 30:2), marriage itself consists of vows and binds the two people together (Ephesians 5:31), therefore I have little reason to overlook the concept of vows or commitments as being a means to create a soul tie". **http://www.greatbiblestudy.com/soulties.php**

We must break off in Jesus' name any ungodly soul ties with people who have a negative influence over us or anyone to whom we have become co-dependent. If we have had an ungodly attraction to a movie star or celebrity or if we have made any object or position into an idol through inordinate affection or selfish ambition, we need to cut off wrong ties in Jesus' name.

As mentioned before, we are not necessarily cutting all soul ties with some people, only the negative ones. If, for instance, we are married and still have a romantic soul tie to someone from our past, we must not only renounce and break those ties off, but we should never keep any mementos such as letters or objects that were given to us by them. If we have maintained an ungodly, romantic soul tie with another person, this is a form of adultery in relation to both our spouse and God. Ungodly affection for others, even fantasy figures, is idolatrous and will diminish relational fulfillment within marriage and with God.

If we have had an unhealthy soul tie to another person, sometimes we will also need to break soul ties from any ungodly 'spirits operating over them.

I am not saying that you can't enjoy a movie star or singer's performance if your connection to them is balanced and healthy. However, there may be times that you will need to take a complete break from contact with someone from the past or from viewing some celebrities or shows. These shows may not have ungodly content in themselves. It is our own emotional responses to them that make them idolatrous or inappropriate for us. This response becomes a blockage to the fruit of the Spirit and receiving wholeness. Something may be a temptation to a person that would never bother another person.

I have noticed today that many people who idolize celebrities have an unhealthy desire to know all about them and their personal lives. Many reality shows are nothing but televised voyeurism. We need to guard our hearts against forming unnatural affections or "inquisitiveness" (**unduly curious about the affairs of others; prying – Webster's Dictionary**) for others that is out of balance with the Spirit of God and therefore becomes an ungodly soul tie. This includes famous Christians who have public ministries.

119

CHAPTER FIFTEEN

The Nature of Human Sexuality

Of all the wonderful gifts that God has given us, human sexuality is one of the most precious. This gift was meant to be the consummation of a loyal, loving, steadfast commitment by a couple toward one another.

The sexual union between a man and woman correlates with God's desire to be intimate with His creation. God desires personal intimacy and connection with His offspring, not religious performance. The correlation between His love and desire for us is expressed in John 14: 20.

> *"On that day you will know that I am in My Father, and you are in Me, and I am in you".*

Without this intimacy with God, we can never fully reflect the love of the Father to others or benefit from the trust and security that the love of God brings to us. We may perform good works, but we may never truly know the Father and we may not be rooted and grounded in love and intimacy with Him.

Matt 7: 22 *"Many will say to Me in that day, 'Lord, Lord, have we not prophesied in Your name, cast out demons in Your name, and done many wonders in Your name?' 23 And then I will declare to them, '**I never knew you;** depart from Me, you who practice lawlessness!'"*

I once heard it said that the word "knew" here in Matt. 7:22 is the very same word in the original Greek language, where it says that Joseph did not "know" Mary until after Christ was born. Relationship with God as with human sexual relationships must be grounded in love, commitment, and faithfulness. Scripture tells us that once we are born again, our bodies are the temple of the Holy Spirit (1 Cor. 6:19) and that we must glorify God in our bodies.

Song of Songs 8:2-3 (TPT) *"I long to bring you to my innermost chamber— this holy sanctuary you have formed within me. O that I might carry you within me! I would give you the spiced wine of my love, this full cup of bliss that we share. We would drink our fill until . . . 3 His left hand cradles my head while his right hand holds me close. We are at rest in this love".*

God desires all human offspring to be conceived from this secure, Godly place of the marriage covenant.

When we misappropriate God's gift of human sexuality, we disqualify ourselves from entering the kingdom of God. This is not to say that these practices are unforgivable sins because there is only one unforgivable sin, which is the blasphemy of the Holy Spirit (Matt. 12:31).

When we come to Christ, if we have been promiscuous in the past, we need to repent of this practice. It's especially important that we break soul ties with every past sexual partner and any spirits attached to their lives and ask the blood of Christ to cleanse us.

The sexual act is not just a joining together of bodies but also a joining of souls, thereby creating a soul-tie with other people.

Soul Ties

"Sex is a tridimensional experience: spirit, soul, and body. Anytime you have sex with a person, you bond with them. Dr. Daniel Amen writes in his book, "Change Your Brain, Change Your Life," "Whenever a person is sexually involved with another person, neurochemical changes occur in both their brains that encourage limbic, emotional bonding. Limbic bonding is the reason casual sex doesn't really work for most people on a whole mind and body level. Two people may decide to have sex 'just for the fun of it,' yet something is occurring on another level that they might not have decided on at all: sex is enhancing an emotional bond between them whether they want it or not. One person, often the woman, is bound to form an attachment and will be hurt when a casual affair ends. One reason it is usually the woman who is hurt most is that the female limbic system is larger than the male's."

This is what we call soul ties. Sex is like gluing two pieces of wood together and the next day ripping them apart. Of course, wood from the opposite board remains on each board. A piece of your sex partner (the good, bad, and ugly) stays with you (and vice versa) for the rest of your life. You can only imagine what it looks like when you bond with multiple partners.

Unhealthy soul ties are often the ramifications of having partners that you create a life-long bond with through a sexual encounter(s), but with whom you only have a short-term relationship with. The bond (soul tie) remains long after the relationship is over, leaving both sexual partners

longing for wholeness". **https://www.moralrevolution.com/
blog/7-signs-of-an-unhealthy-soul-tie**

When we do not have any ability to emotionally relate to people, we are only able to relate to our sexuality as a physical encounter rather than it being relational. So many today see it as nothing more than a cheap thrill, and they will use others for their own lusts without any consideration for them or encountering any sort of deeper relationship. We can never experience the deep satisfaction of the soul that comes from a strong relational commitment and affection for another person unless there is significant healing and restoration.

Many people have tried to fill their empty emotional voids with lustful or shallow relationships that repeatedly fail and leave wounds for all concerned. In doing this, they are looking for another person to fulfill them and that is not possible as no one can fulfill all our needs except God. Oftentimes we believe the lie that a romantic relationship is the highest and best thing in a human being's experience. In doing so, we make this a form of idolatry. This is common these days as so much of music and media revolves around idolizing sex and romance.

> Matthew 5:27 *"You have heard that it was said, 'You shall not commit adultery; 28 but I tell you that everyone who gazes at a woman to lust after her has committed adultery with her already in his heart"*.

Without the Spirit of God dwelling within us, we are powerless to control our bodies and souls' lusts or demands. If we want to have true, meaningful relationships we need to ask God to initialize within us the ability to bond with others and to help us form healthy relationships. We must break off soul ties to past ungodly sexual partners and repent of idolatry and any ungodly fantasies that we have had.

We must then surrender our affections, bodies, and desires to God so that He might have first place in our lives. Communion is a powerful key in bringing death into places where we are in sin. By partaking of the bread, we take the power of the crucified Christ into our souls. The wine (blood of Christ) brings cleansing to our past sins and present lusts. The Spirit of God can then bring transformation and self-control into our thoughts and desires.

"This is also the teaching of Paul in Romans 6, where he says that "our old self was crucified with [Christ]...so that we would no longer be enslaved to sin" (v 6). This is part of Paul's argument for why it is morally incongruous for a believer to continue to live in sin. Christ was crucified for sin (not His, but ours). In His death, "he died to sin, once for all" (v 10), meaning that He died to the judicial power and authority of sin. Since we died with Him, sin has lost its power over us. "So," Paul says, "you also must consider yourselves dead to sin and alive to God in Christ Jesus. Let not sin therefore reign in your mortal body, to make you obey its passions" (vv. 11–12). **https:// servantsofgrace.org/crucified-with-christ-how-the-cross-kills-sin/#:~:text=Christ%20was%20crucified%20for%20 sin%20%28not%20His%2C%20but,Him%2C%20sin%20 has%20lost%20its%20power%20over%20us.**

We must ask the Holy Spirit to initialise and restore to us the capacity for relational bonding and then bring us into the deep, intimate relationship with God that is ours through His love. We need to allow Him to satisfy the areas of our hearts where we have felt emotionally empty and desolate. When we find the true depths of God's love for us, we have a greater capacity to love others.

Marriage is a holy covenant ordained by God for the protection of all human beings, particularly women and children. When we make a marriage commitment before God, His Spirit binds a man and woman's soul together with Himself in a triune covenant. You, your spouse, and God are bound together and all of God's resources become yours within that union.

"In marriage how do the two become one flesh?

God's definition of marriage can be found in Genesis 2:24: "Therefore a man shall leave his father and his mother and hold fast to his wife, and they shall become one flesh." In the Bible, the Hebrew basar is often translated as "flesh," but however it is interpreted, it always refers to the physical part of humanity. What does it mean, then, that a man and woman become "one flesh" in marriage?

The most obvious way is through sex. This is borne out in 1 Corinthians 6:16 when Paul says even a man with a prostitute becomes one flesh with her. The act of sex is a manifestation of "one flesh" physically and a metaphor for the other ways a married couple joins together.

Much of the physical part of life involves maintenance—feeding, housing, and repairing. A man and woman become one flesh in marriage when they share these things as a unit. A man is called to leave his parents—to step out of their home and provision—and become one flesh with his wife. As husband and wife work together in the stuff of life, they become united, and may even start to look like each other.

The flesh is also how we actively respond to what Jesus has done for us. God has prepared good works ahead of time for us to accomplish (Ephesians 2:10). As "one flesh," a married couple coordinates their efforts to ensure they get the work done—both as individuals and as a team. As any couple surrounded by kids, church, work, and friends knows, husbands and wives cannot fulfill their God-given duties unless they work together. **https://www.compelling-truth.org/one-flesh-marriage.html**

Lust or Love?

God intended human sexuality to be conducted in love not lust. Lust is the antithesis of love because it is selfish in nature, and once spent will discard the object of its lust thoughtlessly. Today, society is so programmed by the media to obtain immediate gratification that we fail to see where we break the God-ordained boundaries about our sexuality that are there for our own protection and for our future offspring. Our sexuality besides our spirituality is the most intimate, personal place of a human being. When training our young children, we tell them about their private parts and that no one has the right to touch them inappropriately. However today, for many, once they reach their teens, sexuality becomes a free-for-all without boundaries.

When this happens, we devalue ourselves and others. You wouldn't give someone you've just met your bank account details or the keys to your home or your credit card. How much more valuable is that most personal, intimate place in your life and how much do you value the seed of your own body? No one wants to be brought into the world because of a 'one night stand'. Every human being deserves the dignity of being born into a secure, loving environment that was created with care.

Psalm 127:3 *"Behold, children are a heritage of Yahweh. The fruit of the womb is his reward."*

Beth Saxen

I believe as a society we have lost the value of our sexuality and in doing so have lost the value of our offspring as well. With the same carelessness that human beings are being created, they are now being aborted as worthless objects. Our diminished value of our sexuality leads to a diminished value of humanity itself. When we see a person as a potential "screw" we have not seen their personhood, only someone that we might be able to manipulate for our own personal gratification. This is pure, unadulterated selfishness. It seems that much of society today values being "hot" more than they value being a decent human being. This book is all about foundations and when our sexuality is built upon the wrong foundations, we cannot expect to build healthy relationships in life.

1 John 2:16-17 (NIV) *16 "For everything in the world— the lust of the flesh, the lust of the eyes, and the pride of life—comes not from the Father but from the world. 17 The world and its desires pass away, but whoever does the will of God lives forever".*

Let's look at 1 John 2:16-17 in the Passion Translation

"The love of the Father and the love of the world are incompatible. 16 For all that the world can offer us—the gratification of our flesh, the allurement of the things of the world, and the obsession with status and importance —none of these things come from the Father but from the world. 17 This world and its desires are in the process of passing away, but those who love to do the will of God live forever".

When you see crime in society today you will find that it all pretty much has its roots in the lust of the flesh, lust of the eyes, and the pride of life. When we are driven by lust for power, status, money, or sex, we fail to find a deeper meaning in our lives.

The diminished, shallow values of society leave our offspring without moral guidelines to work within and leave them without respect for themselves or others. They have no understanding of the value of what really matters in life. When we give ourselves over to lust, a spirit of lust will attach itself to our souls and drive us to do things that can either offend our own conscience or conversely it can sear our conscience.

> *"The Bible speaks of a seared conscience in 1 Timothy 4:2. The conscience is the God-given moral conscious-ness within each of us (Romans 2:15). If the conscience is "seared"—literally "cauterized"—then it has been rendered insensitive. Such a conscience does not work properly; it's as if "spiritual scar tissue" has dulled the sense of right and wrong. Just as the hide of an animal scarred with a branding iron becomes numb to further pain, so the heart of an individual with a seared conscience is desensitized to moral pangs".* **https://www.gotquestions. org/seared-conscience.htm**

When a society has not been given foundational values of respect and honor for other people, particularly in the sexual area, we find an alarming increase in sexual violation. We only need to look at the news to see evidence of this. One of the great concerns today is the prevalence of date rape.

Date Rape drugs

> *"Date rape drugs are any type of drug used to make rape or sexual assault easier. Alcohol is often used this way.*

129

1 Or date rape drugs can be put into a drink without you knowing. Drugs or alcohol can make a person confused about what is happening, less able to defend themselves against unwanted sexual contact, or unable to remember what happened. Nearly 11 million women in the United States have been raped while drunk, drugged, or high. 2 If you've been assaulted, it is never your fault". **https://www. womenshealth.gov/a-z-topics/date-rape-drugs**

Children need to be trained regarding the value of their sexuality and the importance of respecting their own bodies and other people's. They need to be taught to guard their hearts from exposure to sexually explicit or pornographic material. Of all the areas that we need to teach our children about self-control in their lives, the issue of controlling their sexual desires is vital. Once we feed sexual lust it can consume us.

Ephesians 4:19 (AMP) *"And they, [the ungodly in their spiritual apathy], having become callous and unfeeling, have given themselves over [as prey] to unbridled sensuality, eagerly craving the practice of every kind of impurity [that their desires may demand]".*

When a person is full of lust, they will look for the most vulnerable prey that they can gain access to. A person must be extremely callous and perverted to abuse young children or elderly people.

"Every week in communities big and small across Australia, children are sexually abused by their relatives.

Leone Shiels, co-ordinator of the Incest Survivors Association, said 78 per cent of the one in three women and one in six men sexually abused before the age of 18, have a relationship with the offender.

> *Australian Bureau of Statistics figures show 43.7 per cent of children sexually abused before the age of 15 are the victims of a male relative, sometimes a father or stepfather."*
>
> **https://www.news.com.au/lifestyle/real-life/the-australian-families-that-hold-dark-secrets-of-incest-and-abuse/news story/7340dbac88e31c194ecada070ad6e997#:~:text=Every%20week%20in%20communities%20big,a%20 relationship%20with%20the%20offender.**

Unfortunately, the church, in the past, has been highly judgmental and condemning people's misuse of their sexuality, viewing it as something 'dirty' rather than seeing it as something precious that is too valuable to sully. Instead of giving people support when they've made mistakes and showing them why God has given us sexual guidelines, the church has judged them. The heart of God cries over human beings who have been diminished and broken by misused sexuality. He does not want the church to rail at sin, but rather to love and teach people the path of light and life. When people wait for a sexual relationship within the boundaries of marriage there is a covering, blessing, and protection for all involved, especially for future offspring.

When we begin a relationship with someone, we are trying to establish whether we are relationally compatible with that person, and this involves taking time to know them. There may be some serious underlying character traits that are not obvious in the initial stages of a relationship that can be revealed over a longer period of time. When we meet and are attracted to someone and then jump into bed with them from the beginning, the sexual side of that act creates a 'bond' so that even though they might not be the right person for us, we form an attachment to them that is not based on 'who' they really are. You can waste a lot of time before you realise that this isn't the direction you want to go. How does a person know if someone really wants a genuine relationship with them or is just using them if they allow themselves to be used? A friend of mine's husband used to say, "Why would you buy the cow when you can get the milk for free?"

I have noticed that when people 'shack up' before they've taken time to really know a person or their character, down the track they break up and several years have passed by pointlessly. This pattern will sometimes repeat itself again and again, and because of this, valuable time will have been wasted in pursuing the wrong relationships. There will always be soul wounds and soul ties attached to these breakups.

I have also noticed many women who have had successive broken relationships that they start to get towards the end of their viable childbearing years and find themselves unattached and concerned about diminishing fertility. When we take time to just know a person first, putting a reign on our sexuality, we will build much more solid foundations for our own lives and our future offspring.

A while back, I saw what was meant to be an artistic photograph of a woman that was supposed to represent the joy of sexual freedom. It was not so much that it was explicit in content as that it was trying to portray how liberated she felt. Personally, I don't believe that there is no such a thing as sexual freedom any more than there is "eating freedom". There isn't much difference between our sexual appetite and our eating appetite. Both have been known to become a form of addiction. No one can eat whatever they want, whenever they want, and as often as they want without becoming ill. We all know that we can eat ourselves into ill health and even death with incorrect eating habits and the same is true of our sexuality. We can develop sexual diseases that can make us ill, leave us infertile, or even kill us.

There isn't one aspect of our bodies that does not require standards and guidelines of truth so that we can stay healthy. Our bodies can only stand certain degrees of temperature before we experience hypothermia or hyperthermia. The quality of the air that we breathe and the food and water that we eat, and drink need to be at a certain level of purity so that we don't become ill. The body requires a balance of specific nutrients so that it can stay healthy. It also needs to have decent quality sleep.

Self-control is such an important aspect of our character. When we practice self-control, this protects us from making big mistakes and enables us to function within healthy guidelines. Just imagine if you weren't disciplined enough to get yourself out of bed in the morning to go to work, or if you were out of control with your spending. People who can't control their mouths frequently get themselves into big trouble too. How much more do we need self-control when it comes to our sexuality? If you can't control yourself, your life will be out of control. Scripture tells us that the fruit of the Spirit of God is self-control (Gal. 5:23).

Proverbs 25:28 (ESV) *"A man without self-control is like a city broken into and left without walls"*.

God's ordained plan for children was for them to be brought up having been wanted from conception and nurtured by two parents who are committed to one another in marriage. No child should ever be conceived through lust. I remember years ago watching one of those shows where people who were adopted early in life, seek to find their real parents once they are adults.

There was a woman who had been adopted into a good family from infancy and who had a good upbringing, however, there was still a deep longing to know where she came from. She wanted to know why she was put up for adoption as a baby, but she also said, "I just want to know that '**I**' wasn't just a one-night stand". Every person has an intrinsic need to know "who" they are, where they came from, and that they were wanted.

When we stay within the protective boundaries of God's guidelines for our sexuality, there is no risk of sexual diseases. Here are some statistics relating to sexual diseases.

Here are some current statistics on STIs

Sexually transmitted infections (STIs)

10 July 2023

Key facts

"More than 1 million sexually transmitted infections (STIs) are acquired every day worldwide, the majority of which are asymptomatic.

Each year there are an estimated 374 million new infections with 1 of 4 curable STIs: chlamydia, gonorrhea, syphilis, and trichomoniasis.

More than 500 million people 15–49 years are estimated to have a genital infection with herpes simplex virus (HSV or herpes) (1).

Human papillomavirus (HPV) infection is associated with over 311,000 cervical cancer deaths each year (2).

Almost 1 million pregnant women were estimated to be infected with syphilis in 2016, resulting in over 350,000 adverse birth outcomes (3).

STIs have a direct impact on sexual and reproductive health through stigmatization, infertility, cancers and pregnancy complications and can increase the risk of HIV.

Drug resistance is a major threat to reducing the burden of STIs worldwide". **https://www.who.int/news-room/ fact-sheets/detail/sexually-transmitted-infections-(stis)#:~:- text=Key%20facts%201%20More%20than%201%20 million%20sexually,simplex%20virus%20%28HSV%20 or%20herpes%29%20%281%29.%20More%20items**

When we look at these statistics, we see that we can pay a high price for sexual "freedom".

I have not presented these statistics to judge people or make them feel guilty. These are clinical facts. Christ died to take away our guilt and shame and heal us from all our wounds whether they were self-inflicted or inflicted by others. We must desire and follow His truth if we want to prosper. God has no desire to condemn people, but we bring ourselves under condemnation when we refuse to follow the light of His Word.

John 3:19 *"And this is the condemnation, that the light has come into the world, and men loved darkness rather than light, because their deeds were evil".*

Anyone at any point can repent and receive God's grace for any sin. It's already paid for, we just need to receive it, but as John 3:19 has shown us, there are some who love the darkness more than light.

Sexual sin profoundly affects us. Because God created our human sexuality as a form of bonding in both body and soul, when we sexually bond with multiple people over a period of years, we can become fragmented in our souls.

Throughout the centuries of mankind's history, the same scenario of women becoming pregnant and abandoned by men has caused untold heartache. People are not toys that we play with for a while and then discard to look for someone else. God is love and

He wants every single person to be treated with love, respect, and honor. We become callous toward others when we "use" people in this way.

I've heard some people say that marriage has become irrelevant these days and that makes me sad because all the finer attributes of human nature must be developed and come into play to create a marriage, a home, and a family. Attributes like fidelity, loyalty, commitment, faithfulness, self-control, and self-sacrifice must be developed in our characters to maintain long-term relationships and a healthy home life. We cannot expect that if we run around giving into our lusts without restraint before we are married that we are automatically going to change and have self-control after we are married.

1 John 2:16 says: *"For all that is in the world—the lust of the flesh, the lust of the eyes, and the pride of life—is not of the Father but is of the world".*

The word "lust" in this Scripture means; longing desire; eagerness to possess or enjoy; unlawful desire of carnal pleasure; evil propensity; depraved affections and desires. **https://www.inspired-walk.com/11901/lust-of-the-flesh-lust-of-the-eyes-pride-of-life**

We cannot build healthy relationships or families when our lusts are out of control.

"Mr. Justice Coleridge, a former family judge in the U.K. with more than 37 years of experience with family law compared the breakdown of family life with being as destructive as the effects of global warming. He described it as a problem that affects all levels of society and that on a daily basis, judges like him witness a "never-ending carnival" of human misery, and that "almost all of society's social

ills can be traced back to the collapse in family stability."
http://www.hizb-ut-tahrir.info/en/index.php/site-sections/
articles/analysis/16124.html

Infatuation does not last

Psychologists say that the initial stage of romantic love where you live on 'cloud nine' usually does not last much more than around two years. They say that romantic relationships generally have an enchantment stage, a disenchantment stage and then if a couple allows their character to grow and they work together, they will move into a maturity stage of lasting value.

How long does infatuation last?

"This phase usually lasts from one to six months but can last as long as two years, or as short as two days. Take it easy in this stage. This is when basic mistakes are made; sound judgement and common sense are having timeout. If you are right for each other you have your lives ahead of you, so what's the rush?

The next stage is back to reality when we start to experience of the reality of love". https://www.agape-aid.org/
relationship-stages/infatuation/

When two people marry, they both bring good character traits and dysfunctional attributes, some of them generational, into their union. With God in our marriages, we will have a much better chance of maturing and coming into wholeness if we remain teachable, prayerful, and open to the direction of the Holy Spirit.

Often, in ministering to someone with sexual problems, whether this may be a form of sexual dysfunction or addiction, we need to look at how they were 'initialised' sexually and at what age. If there has been some sort of childhood abuse, then our sexuality can become skewed and misaligned. This sort of trauma also forms relational blockages to connection and intimacy with others later in life. The response from a trauma like this can either cause someone to be very promiscuous later in life or conversely, they may find themselves with emotional and sexual blockages in their future relationships.

I recall in my childhood that women who could not respond sexually within a relationship were labelled as 'frigid' almost as if it were their identity. I feel fairly certain that some sort of sexual wounding or trauma will have taken place during their lifetime that has shut down that God-given part of their humanity.

If someone has suffered childhood sexual abuse, they have been violated at the deepest level of their personhood. Their most personal boundaries have been breached. To abuse someone in this way is to treat them as though they are worthless and that have no rights. Children internalise this. So, we need to minister to them by the Spirit of God and ask Him to re-establish healthy identity and restore their boundaries correctly within them.

Physical Symptoms of Childhood Sexual Abuse

- *Chronic pelvic pain*
- *Gastrointestinal symptoms/distress*
- *Musculoskeletal complaints*
- *Obesity, eating disorders*
- *Insomnia, sleep disorders*
- *Pseudocyesis*
- *Sexual dysfunction*
- *Asthma, respiratory ailments*
- *Addictions (alcohol addiction/ drug addiction)*
- *Chronic headache*

- *Chronic back pain*
- *Psychological and Behavioral Symptoms of Childhood Sexual Abuse*
- *Depression and anxiety*
- *Posttraumatic stress disorder symptoms*
- *Dissociative states*
- *Repeated self-injury*
- *Suicide attempts*
- *Lying, stealing, truancy, running away*
- *Poor contraceptive practices*
- *Compulsive sexual behaviors*
- *Sexual dysfunction*
- *Somatizing disorders*
- *Eating disorders*
- *Poor adherence to medical recommendations*
- *Intolerance of or constant search for intimacy*
- *Expectation of early death*

**https://www.healthyplace.com/abuse/articles/
symptoms-adult-survivors-childhood-sexual-abuse**

Only God can heal the heart and soul so that we can have a healthy relationship with Him, ourselves, and others.

CHAPTER SIXTEEN

Seeking God's Love in Recovery

In dealing with any area of dysfunction, the beginning of recovery is to first acknowledge that we have problems and to be committed to our own recovery.

Seeking God should be a part of every believer's life. Hebrews 11:6 (KJV) says;

> *"But without faith it is impossible to please him: for he that cometh to God must believe that he is, and that he is a rewarder of them that diligently seek him".*

We are taught as Christians to "abide in Christ" by staying in prayer and by meditating upon the Word of God. This is great for the maintenance of our relationship with God, but when we want to press in deeper in our relationship with God or have special needs or when we have a desire for keys for a breakthrough in a specific area of our lives, there is another dimension of fasting and prayer. This involves making special trysting places with the Lord where we fast, pray, and delegate a more elongated period of time to spend in His presence. We can seek God for a deeper relationship with Him and for a greater ability to connect more with

His Father's heart. Seeking is not *striving* but instead *choosing* to prioritise making yourself available to God and to also finding specific keys that will assist us in our recovery.

> Jeremiah 29:13-14 (KJV) *"And ye shall seek me, and find me, when ye shall search for me with all your heart. 14 And I will be found of you, saith the Lord: and I will turn away your captivity, and I will gather you from all the nations, and from all the places whither I have driven you, saith the Lord; and I will bring you again into the place whence I caused you to be carried away captive".*

Seeking God and His kingdom also involves getting ministry from those who specialize in inner healing.

Addressing our accumulation of negative baggage can be a very ugly, confronting thing. He wants to take us on a journey of healing and recovery that will lead us into the fulfillment of all that He has promised us in Christ. The first thing that we need to know in a relationship with Christ is that there is no condemnation for those that belong to Him and that "we are *accepted* in the beloved" (Eph. 1:6). The word '*accepted*' in the Greek occurs one other time in the New Testament, where the angel Gabriel said to Mary.

> Luke 1:28 (KJV) *"Hail, thou that art highly **favoured**, (accepted) the Lord is with thee: blessed art thou among women".*

No matter what stage of recovery you are at, you are always accepted and loved.

God is all about love. His word tells us in John 15:9 (KJV), *"As the Father has loved me, so have I loved you. Continue ye in my love"*. God wants to recompense us for all the years that we lacked love and nurture.

Sometimes we can feel unlovable, but our Heavenly Father knows where we came from, and He is so glad that we belong to Him and is excited about our recovery and He is committed to the long haul. It takes time to be perfected in love.

We often say that we would like to get closer to God, but in truth, we can't get any closer to Him because scripture tells us in Ephesians 2:*13:*

> *"But now in Christ Jesus you who once were far away **have been brought near** by the blood of Christ"*. (emphasis mine)

Positionally, we have been given the gift of nearness and acceptance by the Father. This nearness is our birthright in Christ.

God has justified us because of our faith in Christ, not because of our performance. Romans 4:3 (NIV) says;

> *". . . Abraham believed God, and it was credited to him as righteousness."*

Many of us have never known the intimacy of parental love so our senses are not trained towards intimacy. Hebrews 5:14 speaks about having our senses and mental faculties trained so that we can discern spiritual truths. Accepting God's love and nearness is another area that we need to "train our senses" so that we become more attuned to His presence within our lives.

Christ did not just give Himself **for** us, He gave Himself **to** us. I remember at one stage of my life saying to Him, "Lord I know that you are my treasure, my greatest gift. Please help me to see you and value you as I should. We need to seek His heart and not just His hand and what He can do for us. My greatest joy when I wake up in the morning is that He is there, being proactive and enthusiastic about our day together. This has changed my perspective on life in so many ways.

Jesus said, 'Live or abide within my love', (John 15:9 NLT). God's love towards us is unconditional and unchanging and this love must be the foundation upon which we stand on this journey of recovery. His love is where we have been planted and where we must allow ourselves to become rooted and grounded in Him. Even before we are perfected, God calls us trees of righteousness, the planting of the Lord (Isaiah 61:3). His love is like the nutrients that nourish a plant and cause it to thrive. His light is like the sunshine that sustains and imparts energy to a plant.

> Ephesians 3:16-18 (NIV) *"I pray that out of his glorious riches he may strengthen you with power through his Spirit in your inner being, 17 so that Christ may dwell in your hearts through faith. And I pray that you, being rooted and established in love, 18 may have power, together with all the Lord's holy people, to grasp how wide and long and high and deep is the love of Christ. . ."*

> 1 John 4:18-19 (NIV) *"There is no fear in love, but perfect love drives out fear, because fear involves punishment. The one who fears has not been perfected in love. 19We love Him because He first loved us".*

In years gone by, much of the religious teaching was based on the performance of the law and fear of punishment if we failed, but this is not scriptural. God "punished" Christ upon the cross on our behalf and there is now no anger left in Him towards us when we are in Christ. He will discipline us, however He never disciplines us in anger, but always with lovingkindness and with our benefit in mind. If we feel unloved and unworthy to approach the Lord, then this does not come from God but from the rejection within our souls or false religious teaching. These things hinder us from receiving the revelation of God's love from the Spirit of God and we must deal with them.

Overcoming this frequently involves dealing with images of parental, or authority figures in our lives and how we think that they see us. If they were abusive or indifferent towards us, chances are that we would have a blockage in receiving the truth about the character and nature of God. We must renounce the lies that we believed from our past and then declare the truth. For instance, we can renounce the lie that Father God is like our natural father or any authority figures that hurt or neglected us. If we don't undo these concepts, they will remain within our souls and "clash" with the truth of what God's love is like and what His heart truly is towards us. Until we do this, we will be vulnerable to being perfor-mance-driven by fear of failure and therefore unable to experience the fullness of God's love. If we have fear, we are not yet perfected in love.

"Date: June 12, 2012 Source: Society for Personality and Social Psychology Summary: A father's love contributes as much—and sometimes more—to a child's development as does a mother's love. That is one of many findings in a new large-scale analysis of research about the power of paren-tal rejection and acceptance in shaping our personalities as children and into adulthood.

In our half-century of international research, we've not found any other class of experience that has as strong and consistent effect on personality and personality devel-opment as does the experience of rejection, especially by parents in childhood," says Ronald Rohner of the University of Connecticut, co-author of the new study in Personality and Social Psychology Review. "Children and adults everywhere—regardless of differences in race, culture, and gender—tend to respond in exactly the same way when they perceived themselves to be rejected by their caregivers and other attachment figures." **https://www.sciencedaily.com/ releases/2012/06/120612101338.htm – Father's love is one of the greatest influences on personality development**

We can carry a spirit of grief, disappointment, and desolation when our childhood lacked emotional nurture. For some, those soul deficits and disconnection can be their paradigm of "normality". I believe that God placed all the attributes of His love and nature in both the father and mother. Lack of parental love and validation leaves a deficit in our own sense of identity and ability to be able to relate well to others.

We must ask Holy Spirit for revelation of the truth of God's unconditional love and awareness of His constant presence, so that we have a firm foundation to walk upon as we journey toward our recovery. Christ promised us that He would never leave us or forsake us (Heb. 13:5) and that there is no condemnation in Him towards us. These promises provide us with a sense of stability so that when we fail, we don't need to feel ashamed or condemned by Him. This makes it so much easier for us to repent, pick ourselves up, and continue walking with Him toward our recovery and our future inheritance. He doesn't look at us and say, "I hope that they don't make a mistake today", nor does He expect perfection from us. He knows where each of us came from, and He patiently walks and works with us. When we fail, we can use our mistakes as objective lessons to avoid falling into the same pitfalls again. If God loved us even before we came to Him, He will not forsake us now that we belong to Him.

Romans 5:8 NIV *"But God demonstrates his own love for us in this: While we were still sinners, Christ died for us"*.

A common stumbling block in our recovery can be when we compare ourselves to others. We might see other Christians that seem shiny and squeaky clean but many times they may have had very different foundations from us and have begun life from a much greater vantage point. Comparisons will undermine us and keep our focus on ourselves and our performance when our eyes must always be fixed upon our Saviour. There is no performance in God, but instead, we rely upon the work of the cross and the grace and power of the Holy Spirit to transform us. There's an old Hymn that states, "Nothing in my hands I bring, but simply to the cross I cling". God works best in still vessels, when we cease our efforts and strivings and rely totally upon Him to change us.

There are times when you can have prayer ministry to a particular area of brokenness, and something will break through instantly and never bother you again. There are, however, other times when a certain struggle can come up repeatedly over a certain issue and this will require perseverance to get your breakthrough. This can be because there can be many layers of memories of the same type, such as rejection, which are held in a stronghold by the enemy. It may also take time to process all unforgiveness in relation to those wounds.

I knew a young woman whose mother told her that her conception was "an accident" and that she was never wanted. This young woman became very promiscuous in her teens because she was looking for the love that she was denied by her parents. In a situation like this, the power of the spoken word must be broken off as well as the negative soul ties to the person who spoke to them before we ask the Holy Spirit to minister healing to every place where this situation impacted us negatively. Again, repenting of any of our own attitudes towards those that hurt us.

In this young woman's case, she would also need to renounce the lie that she would find fulfillment for her love deficit by sleeping around and then ask God to reveal His love and fill all those empty, barren places within her soul. She would then need to cut soul ties to the people from the past with whom she'd had ungodly, sexual relationships with and break off all negative spirits attached to them.

We must seek God for the revelation of where there are any blockages that hinder us from receiving His love because without His love we cannot grow.

CHAPTER SEVENTEEN

The Weapons of Our Warfare

There are many keys to recovery and weapons of warfare that we can use to break free from multiple layers of foundational strongholds. We need to have a strong foundation in the Word of God and develop the practice of spiritual warfare. We also need to have a well-developed personal prayer life so that we are equipped to work through some of our personal issues. But at the end of the day, we must be led by the Spirit as to what keys we need to specifically apply to each specific situation. I once heard someone say, "Pray before you pray". I often anoint myself with oil before I pray asking the Holy Spirit to anoint me with revelation and discernment as well as wisdom and direction to pray effectively. I also pray that my mind, heart, eyes, and ears be attuned to the voice of His Spirit.

Ephesians 6:10-18 (NIV) speaks about The Armor of God:

"10 Finally, be strong in the Lord and in his mighty power. 11 Put on the full armor of God, so that you can take your stand against the devil's schemes. 12 For our struggle is not against flesh and blood, but against the rulers, against the authorities, against the powers of this dark world and

against the spiritual forces of evil in the heavenly realms. 13 Therefore put on the full armor of God, so that when the day of evil comes, you may be able to stand your ground, and after you have done everything, to stand. 14 Stand firm then, with the belt of truth buckled around your waist, with the breastplate of righteousness in place, 15 and with your feet fitted with the readiness that comes from the gospel of peace. 16 In addition to all this, take up the shield of faith, with which you can extinguish all the flaming arrows of the evil one. 17 Take the helmet of salvation and the sword of the Spirit, which is the word of God. 18 And pray in the Spirit on all occasions with all kinds of prayers and requests. With this in mind, be alert and always keep on praying for all the Lord's people ".

The word of God is the sword of the Spirit. This is an offensive weapon against the enemy. Jesus used the Word of God to refute the enemies' lies when He was enduring the wilderness temptation. Every time the enemy tempted Him, He answered, "No, for the Word of God says..."

The shield of faith is a defensive weapon when we're under attack. We can use our faith to quench all the fiery darts of the enemy. In most battles, we need both weapons. However, to use these weapons out of our own understanding and strength would be the equivalent of pulling out the cutlery drawer, picking up an implement at random, and brandishing it in the enemy's face as a weapon. In every situation, we need to know what our current weapon of warfare is, and we need the anointing and discernment of the Spirit to apply it.

Ephesians 6:16-17 KJV "Above all, taking the shield of faith, wherewith ye shall be able to quench all the fiery

*darts of the wicked. 17 And take the helmet of salvation,
and the sword of the Spirit, which is the word of God:"*

When David slew Goliath, his divinely appointed weapon was
a sling and some stones. The power to overcome his giant wasn't
really in David or the weapon itself, but rather it was in God's
anointing upon him and on God's designated weapon of warfare
that gave David power to overcome as he moved in obedience
to God.

Samson slew a thousand Philistines with the Jawbone of an
axe. Nowhere else in the Old Testament does it refer to anyone
else using these implements or strategies to wage war against their
enemies. This is why we need to have discernment in our prayer
lives. We need to know how the Holy Spirit is leading us and what
to apply at any given time. God does not want us to put work out
of method or to rely merely on principles of faith in warfare. Our
ability to hear the Spirit and be led by what He is saying gives us
our most effective stance in warfare or deliverance. This requires
intimacy with God which attunes us to see and hear His voice and
leading. Over the years I've noticed that the people who make the
best recovery from poor foundations, spend a lot of personal time
with God as well as having consistent external ministry support.

Years ago, I was waiting on the Lord for something that I can't
specifically recall now, but I was asking Him what my weapons of
warfare were in that situation. As I was waiting, I had the impres-
sion that I was holding in my hands some sort of clay pot that
contained oil. So, I asked the Lord what that was about, and He
said to me, "The anointing oil breaks the yoke of bondage" (Isaiah
10:27). So, I sat and received the grace of the Holy Spirit into that
issue that I was praying about. Just because God does something
one way on one occasion, does not mean that He will do it the same
way the next time.

Praise is a weapon

When Joshua obeyed the Lord's command to walk around the fortified city of Jericho, the musicians and singers went before the warriors, blew their trumpets, and proclaimed the power of God. Those walls around the city were wide enough for men to ride chariots upon them, but when the Israelites obeyed God's particular strategy, the walls collapsed down into the ground. Praise and thanksgiving are very powerful means of warfare and by giving praise to God in a difficult situation, we release His presence into our circumstances and against our enemies.

There were times in the Old Testament when God would send out the musicians and singers before His army and their praise alone scattered the enemy. At other times He spoke to His people when they were confronting an enemy and He would say, "Stand still and you will see the salvation of the Lord" (Exodus 14:13; 2 Chronicles 20:17). Sometimes when we have done all we can do, He will direct us to just stand (Eph. 6:13).

There were also times that He would tell them to go and fight the battle and He would promise them that He would give them great victory. We can see from these different situations that we need the revelation and direction of the Spirit of God for our battle strategy, to take ground back from the enemy.

Sometimes, the enemy will come out of left field and bring an attack against us that we aren't equipped to conquer with our current level of faith or weaponry. When this happens, we must pursue God with all our might for new revelations and strategies of warfare. We need to receive an upgrade on our current 'arsenal', and revelation of the correct application of these weapons to be able to withstand and conquer the current 'Goliath' that we are facing. For instance, if we are confronted with a life-threatening situation in our health or our family's health and we have never battled or conquered a giant like this before, then we need to be fasting, praying, and seeking God for an upgrade in wisdom and discernment and for anointing and keys for spiritual warfare.

Keys

Jesus spoke about the keys of the kingdom in Matthew 16:19 (NIV). He said,

"I will give you the keys of the kingdom of heaven; whatever you bind on earth will be bound in heaven, and whatever you loose on earth will be loosed in heaven."

We use these keys of binding and loosing in the name of Jesus so that we can advance the kingdom of God. He wants us to loose people from the power of the enemy and bind them into healing, recovery, and wholeness.

Because Christ was obedient to God, even submitting Himself to death upon the cross, God has given him all authority on heaven and earth and His name enforces that authority.

Philippians 2:9-10 (NIV) *"Therefore God exalted him to the highest place and gave him the name that is above every name, that at the name of Jesus every knee should bow, in heaven and on earth and under the earth . . ."*

Jesus delegated the gift of the authority of His Name, to His disciples and to future believers to enable them to displace the works of darkness and to enforce the kingdom of God. Didn't Jesus teach us to pray, "thy kingdom come, thy will be done on earth as it is in heaven"? To enforce His will on earth we must know the authority of Jesus' name.

John 16: 23-24 (NIV) *"In that day you will no longer ask
me anything. Very truly I tell you, my Father will give you
whatever you ask in my name. 24 Until now you have not
asked for anything in my name. Ask and you will receive,
and your joy will be complete"*.

All Christians will experience external battles with circumstances throughout their lives, however, a great deal of the battles
we face are also in our own minds. Emotional programming and
wounds from the past can form our own "virtual reality", of how
we see things in life, as well as how we think others see us. The
enemy attaches himself to our past pain and these wounds are like
"lenses" that "colour" the way that we see life. In dealing with this,
firstly we need to identify the lies of the enemy before we can deal
with them. We then need to break off and renounce agreements
with these spirits and their lying deceptions and ask the Holy Spirit
to show us the truth wherever we have been deceived.

Deficits such as a lack of identity and self-worth leave us vulnerable to lies and deception. Parents initialize a sense of connection
to others, self-worth, identity, and initiative within a child so if this
has been neglected there will be parts of us that have never been
activated and remain dormant. We may carry an "orphan spirit"
where we do not feel a sense of belonging and many people can
almost feel like they are invisible. To address this, we must first
deal with any strongholds, thoughts, and emotions before we call
upon the love and power of the Holy Spirit to initialize and awaken
these "receptors" that enable us to feel identity and worth and to
connect us to God and others. Dwelling upon the Word of God and
those scriptures that relate to the Father heart of God is a powerful weapon to cut through the lies of the enemy and replace them
with truth. As previously mentioned, in all healing and recovery,
we must displace a negative first before we replace it with healing
and truth.

Eph.1:4-5 (NIV) *"For he chose us in him before the creation of the world to be holy and blameless in his sight. 5 In love he predestined us for adoption to sonship through Jesus Christ, in accordance with his pleasure and will".*

Proactive responses during battle

Often in my early days, when I was facing a battle, I would become so frustrated with God that I would respond in anger. I would feel that He was not helping me and that I was alone and abandoned. These reactions were obviously coming from unresolved wounds and lies within my soul. As I matured in the Lord, I had to learn to be proactive in my responses to pressure. I learned how to use self-control over my feelings and to declare who God was to me during difficult times. I consciously decided to confess His promises over me, rather than venting every thought and emotion that I was feeling.

Proverbs 29:11 (KJV) *"A fool uttereth all his mind: but a wise man keepeth it in till afterwards".*

Never let your emotions control you during a difficult time. Always use the word of God as a guideline for all your attitudes and responses just as Christ did in the wilderness temptation. This is what it means to walk in the Spirit and not in the flesh. We will never gain victory in any situation by venting negative thoughts and emotions. This is the process that Jesus referred to when He said we must "die to self". He was not saying we obliterate our normal, God-given human personality and traits, but only that which is negative and misaligned with the Word and promises of God.

Keep sowing in your battle

Our journey to wholeness can be long and require much endurance. During our battle towards freedom, we must regularly take time to receive refreshment and encouragement from the Lord. However, one of the most important aspects of overcoming is to steadfastly sow whatever we want to reap. If we sow negative responses as I've just touched on, we are not going to reap anything good from it. Ask the Holy Spirit to show you how to keep on pursuing and pressing through without striving in your own flesh. As the Apostle Paul told us, we must keep running the race of faith and pressing towards the prize of God's inheritance for us. (Phil. 2:14)

> Psalm 126 (KJV) *1 "When the Lord turned again the captivity of Zion, we were like them that dream.*
>
> *2 Then was our mouth filled with laughter, and our tongue with singing: then said they among the heathen, The Lord hath done great things for them.*
>
> *3 The Lord hath done great things for us; whereof we are glad.*
>
> *4 Turn again our captivity, O Lord, as the streams in the south.*
>
> *5 They that sow in tears shall reap in joy.*
>
> *6 He that goeth forth and weepeth, bearing precious seed, shall doubtless come again with rejoicing, bringing his sheaves with him".*

If we sow well by making pro-active choices during times of weeping, we will reap a harvest of freedom and victory.

God has sown much seed within us, and we have sown the seed for breakthrough into others through love and prayers. Sometimes it seems to take so long to receive the answers, but I encourage you to persevere. Do not despair if you haven't seen the answers to all your prayers yet, it is on the way.

CHAPTER EIGHTEEN

The Blood of Christ – The Resurrection Power of The Spirit of God – The Word of Our Testimony

The power of the blood of Christ, His broken body, and His resurrection power are vital keys to our receiving cleansing, healing, and transformation within the soul. Scripture says that if we confess our sins, the blood of Christ cleanses us from all unrighteousness.

> Hebrews 9:14, (NIV) *"How much more, then, will the blood of Christ, who through the eternal Spirit offered himself unblemished to God, cleanse our consciences from acts that lead to death, so that we may serve the living God"!*

The blood of Christ is a powerful legal weapon in spiritual warfare because it represents the covenant that we entered into with God when we received Christ as Saviour. It is also cleansing and healing to every part of our beings. Speaking of overcoming the devil, Revelations 12:11 (NIV) says,

"They triumphed over him by the blood of the Lamb and by the word of their testimony; they did not love their lives so much as to shrink from death".

The shed blood of Christ cancelled the enemy's power to have a right of access to us. When we stand upon the power of the blood of the Lamb, we are declaring a legal transaction that redeemed us from all the power of the kingdom of darkness and gave us victory over the enemy.

Right throughout the history of mankind, in every culture no matter how advanced or primitive it may be, there has always been a system of law. There are lawgivers and law enforcers and those who judge people who break the law and set a penalty for whatever act was committed against the law.

Every person who has been wronged always wants to see justice served for whatever wrong they have suffered. It is the same in God's kingdom.

Scripture tells us *"For the wages of sin is death; but the gift of God is eternal life through Jesus Christ our Lord".* Romans 6:23 (KJV)

Christ was the sacrificial Lamb who bore the payment for our sins upon the cross. If He had been a sinful man, His suffering would have been justly deserved, but because He was without sin, He was able to offer Himself on our behalf as payment for our sins. The prophet Isaiah tells us that it was because of the stripes (lashes) of Christ that we have healing available to us as well as forgiveness of sins.

Isaiah 53:1-12 (NIV) *"Who has believed our message and to whom has the arm of the Lord been revealed? 2 He grew up before him like a tender shoot, and like a root out of dry ground. He had no beauty or majesty to attract us to him, nothing in his appearance that we should desire him. 3 He was despised and rejected by mankind, a man of suffering, and familiar with pain. Like one from whom people hide their faces he was despised, and we held him in low esteem. 4 Surely, he took up our pain and bore our suffering, yet we considered him punished by God, stricken by him, and afflicted.*

5 But he was pierced for our transgressions, he was crushed for our iniquities; the punishment that brought us peace was on him, and by his wounds we are healed.

6 We all, like sheep, have gone astray, each of us has turned to our own way; and the Lord has laid on him the iniquity of us all.

7 He was oppressed and afflicted, yet he did not open his mouth; he was led like a lamb to the slaughter, and as a sheep before its shearers is silent, so he did not open his mouth.

8 By oppression and judgment he was taken away. Yet who of his generation protested? For he was cut off from the land of the living; for the transgression of my people he was punished.

9 He was assigned a grave with the wicked, and with the rich in his death, though he had done no violence, nor was any deceit in his mouth.

10 Yet it was the Lord's will to crush him and cause him to suffer, and though the Lord makes his life an offering for sin, he will see his offspring and prolong his days, and the will of the Lord will prosper in his hand.

11 After he has suffered, he will see the light of life and be satisfied; by his knowledge my righteous servant will justify many, and he will bear their iniquities.

12 Therefore I will give him a portion among the great, and he will divide the spoils with the strong, because he poured out his life unto death, and was numbered with the transgressors. For he bore the sin of many, and made inter-cession for the transgressors".

Christ paid the full price for our sin upon the cross and through the whipping that He endured by the Roman soldiers, all our sickness, griefs and sorrows were carried away. His head was pierced with the crown of thorns so that we could have a sound mind, the chastisement of our peace was upon Him.

This is why Jesus said that He was the door to the Father and that there is no other way for us to approach God. There was a legal transaction that took place at the cross that God provided, and we cannot pick and choose how we approach Him.

John 10: 1 *"Then Jesus said, Believe me when I tell you that anyone who does not enter the sheepfold though the door, but climbs in by some other way, is a thief and a rogue. It is the shepherd of the flock who goes in by the door. It is to him the door-keeper opens the door and it is his voice that the sheep recognise".*

We cannot access God or His Kingdom's gifts of healing and deliverance through any other means than through the Person of Christ.

When we have an ingrained habit of sin that has been ongoing for a long time, we need to spend time soaking in the presence of God. We can claim the blood of Christ over our wounds and sin in our hearts. It is enormously powerful to take communion over the specific areas where we need victory, declaring Christ's death into our ungodly responses, His cleansing power over them by the blood, and the resurrection power of the Spirit to transform them.

We can soak in the resurrection power of the Holy Spirit, quietly receiving His grace. We can also apply the Word of God by confessing scriptures that pertain to our area of need.

Job 22:28 (KJV) *"Thou shalt also decree a thing, and it shall be established unto thee: and the light shall shine upon thy ways".*

There are several good books out there relating to 'soul declarations' that are based on scripture which are very powerful, and these can be helpful in our recovery. We declare His Word over ourselves and look to His grace and the power of the Spirit of God abiding within us to transform us. By using these powerful keys, we are putting off our old nature and putting on the new nature.

Ephesians 4:22-24 (KJV) *"22 That ye put off concerning the former conversation the old man, which is corrupt according to the deceitful lusts; 23 And be renewed in the spirit of your mind; 24 And that ye put on the new man, which after God is created in righteousness and true holiness".*

The resurrection power of the Spirit of God transforms us into newness of life. The same Spirit that raised Christ from the dead resides within us when we are born again.

Romans 6:4 (NIV) *"We therefore were buried with Him through baptism into death, in order that, just as Christ was raised from the dead through the glory of the Father, we too may walk in newness of life".*

Romans 6:7-9 (NIV) *"because anyone who has died has been set free from sin. 8 Now if we died with Christ, we believe that we will also live with him. 9 For we know that since Christ was raised from the dead, he cannot die again; death no longer has mastery over him".*

Our transformation is appropriated by faith in the work of the cross and the resurrection power of Christ. It is not attained by our own efforts.

1 John 3:8 (KJV) *"For this purpose the Son of God was manifested, that he might destroy the works of the devil".*

There is no striving in Christ and nothing from our own efforts can bring about the changes that we need within. This must be a surrendering to the work of divine grace. Without realizing the power of the Spirit and the cross in our lives, many Christians will habitually go through the negative cycle of repenting before God and telling Him that they won't do that thing again, and then turning around and repeating the same thing over and over. For those with a powerless, religious spirit, there will always be a sense of shame and failure attached to this.

Romans 1:16: (KJV) says *"For I am not ashamed of the gospel of Christ: for it is the **power** (emphasis mine) of God unto salvation to everyone that believeth; to the Jew first, and also to the Greek".*

When we are working towards transformation in an area of our lives, we rest in Christ's unconditional love for us regardless of our behavior. We stand in confession of the word of God, the work of the cross, and faith in the power of God at work within us and not upon our own personal performance.

Without the power of Christ's death and His resurrection Spirit dwelling within us, we have a powerless gospel. If the only hope that we have to be changed is in what we can accomplish by ourselves, then we wouldn't need a Saviour. This is why Romans 8:37 (NIV) says;

"No, in all these things we are more than conquerors through him who loved us. 38 For I am convinced that neither death nor life, neither angels nor demons, neither the present nor the future, nor any powers, 39 neither height nor depth, nor anything else in all creation, will be able to separate us from the love of God that is in Christ Jesus our Lord".

God's Word contains inheritance promises that we must 'claim' by quoting and declaring in faith, those things which He says are ours. Otherwise, it is like we have an inheritance deposited in a bank account in heaven that we never draw from and therefore remain poor in spirit. When we draw from this deposit of His promises and from His Spirit abiding within us, we are drawing from what Scripture refers to as the wells of salvation. Isaiah 12:3 (KJV) says, *"Therefore with joy shall ye draw water out of the wells of salvation".*

2 Peter 1:3-8 (NIV) *"His divine power has given us everything we need for a godly life through our knowledge of him who called us by his own glory and goodness. 4 Through these he has given us his very great and precious promises, so that through them you may participate in the divine nature, having escaped the corruption in the world caused by evil desires. 5 For this very reason, make every effort to add to your faith goodness; and to goodness, knowledge; 6 and to knowledge, self-control; and to self-control, perseverance; and to perseverance, godliness; 7 and to godliness, mutual affection; and to mutual affection, love. 8 For if you possess these qualities in increasing measure,*

*they will keep you from being ineffective and unproductive
in your knowledge of our Lord Jesus Christ".*

Instead of living in the constant cycle of performance and
defeat, we can claim by faith the promise that we are partakers
of the divine nature, as we just read in 2 Peter 1:4. We have been
given great and precious promises of God to always draw from.

2 Corinthians 9:8 (NIV) *"And God is able to bless you
abundantly, so that in all things at all times, having all that
you need, you will abound in every good work".*

In this, we see that Christ truly is our all-sufficiency. So how do
we experience this in reality? We must persistently apply the power
of the death of Christ upon the cross to all sin and bad habits. This
includes any ungodly identifications, associations, affiliations, or
affections. By faith, we replace these things with the power of the
Spirit and His righteousness and confess by faith all the promises
of God that relate to whatever current battle we are facing.

When God commissioned Joshua to go and possess the
Promised Land, this was His instructions:

Joshua 1:8 (NIV) *"Keep this Book of the Law always on
your lips; meditate on it day and night, so that you may
be careful to do everything written in it. Then you will be
prosperous and successful".*

Speaking the word of God over ourselves, others and circumstances is like planting seeds. If we want to move mountains in our
lives, declaration of the word of God is one of the keys that will
assist our recovery.

Matthew 17:20 (NIV) *"...Truly I tell you, if you have faith as small as a mustard seed, you can <u>say</u> to this mountain, 'Move from here to there,' and it will move. Nothing will be impossible for you."*

Christ paid the highest price, in shedding His own blood for us. His broken body and His shed blood was the price that He paid for our redemption from the kingdom of darkness and the power of sin. When we come to the communion table, we come in an act of remembrance and honour to the Lamb of God. We also come to a place where there is a feast prepared for us.

Song of Solomon 2:4 (KJV) *"He brought me to the banqueting house, and his banner over me was love".*

Even when we are in a battle, all the provisions of the table of Christ are available to us.

Psalm 23:5 (NIV) *"You prepare a table before me in the presence of my enemies. You anoint my head with oil; my cup overflows".*

This table of provisions grants us every resource of discernment, wisdom, and direction as to how to stand and what specific weapons apply to our situation. There are also refreshments to be had here when we are weary.

God wants us to lay claim to the provisions of His promises for us. Can you imagine how Christ would feel, after paying the high price of dying upon the cross for our redemption, when He sees His people not taking hold of these gifts or receiving by faith those things that were won by His sacrifice?

When there is a death, a will goes into action. God has given us an inheritance that was activated when Christ died upon the cross for us. Because of the Spirit of Adoption that we received at salvation; we can lay claim to our inheritance in Christ.

If we do not know the Word of God and His promises, then we are ignorant of our inheritance so we can still live like we are poor orphans. We need to understand the power, privileges, and responsibilities that we have been given as Sons of God to be fulfilled in life and to fulfill His Kingdom's purpose on this earth.

Romans 8:32 (NIV) *"He who did not spare his own Son, but gave him up for us all—how will he not also, along with him, graciously give us all things?"*

CHAPTER NINETEEN

The Wells of Salvation

If we have become weary on our healing journey, we can invite the Holy Spirit into those places where we are feeling dry, barren, and discouraged. Sometimes it feels as if the journey is taking so long but it's important that we accept the Lord's timing in our progress.

> Isaiah 12:3-5 (KJV) *"Therefore with joy you will draw water from the wells of salvation".*

If you're feeling tired or overwhelmed, it is good to just sit and receive from God. We can begin to enter His presence by thanking Him for the deposit of His Spirit within. Thank Him for a sound and quiet mind. Ask Him to help you to have a heart to receive. You will feel His peace and presence rise within you, as you begin to draw the resources of His Spirit, into your weary soul. Whatever you feel that you lack, draw it up by faith and confession from the wells of salvation.

> Corinthians 9:8 (NIV) *"And God is able to make all grace abound to you, so that in all things, **at all times**, (emphasis*

mine) having all that you need, you will abound in every good work".

Draw from the presence of the Holy Spirit residing within you and surrender afresh to His timing. Draw from God's resources and keep on doing this until you see a change in your attitude and heart. Allow His grace to flow into angry, bitter, offended, or prideful places. Whatever you need, draw it from His indwelling presence.

In John 5 we see an analogy of the wellsprings of God.

John 5:4 (KJV*) "For an angel went down at a certain season into the pool, and troubled the water: whosoever then first after the troubling of the water stepped in was made whole of whatsoever disease he had".*

The sick and infirmed would wait beside the pool of Bethesda and when the angel stirred up the water a healing anointing was released, then, whoever stepped into the pool first received his/ her healing. The man that Jesus healed at the pool had been lame for a long time because, when the water was stirred, he was physically unable to enter before anyone else. But we can enter God's anointing at any time, even in those moments when our soul feels like fainting, we can "stir up" the anointing by praising, singing, and quoting scriptures. This is the last thing that we feel like doing when we are feeling flat, but it is exactly what we need to do. We don't have to be loud and emphatic, even if all we can manage is a whisper it is still powerful.

We have all been in worship sessions where we sense a strong anointing of the Spirit as we give God praise and honor and worship. This is because we release the anointing of worship from our inner man and because God responds to the praise of His people.

Psalm 22:3 (AMPC) *"But You are holy, O You Who dwell in [the holy place where] the praises of Israel [are offered]"*

It was God's intention that we live our lives by drawing our resources from the stream of life within us.

John 7:37-38 (NIV) *"On the last and greatest day of the festival, Jesus stood and said in a loud voice, "Let anyone who is thirsty come to me and drink. 38 Whoever believes in me, as Scripture has said, rivers of living water will flow from within them."*

In the Middle East in Old Testament times, water was their most valuable commodity. When an enemy wished to attack another tribe of people, one of their strategies was to throw rocks, rubble, and even dead animals into their wells to contaminate their water supply. This is an analogy of what the enemy tries to do to 'wellspring' of our soul so that the fruit of the Spirit cannot be released through us.

The enemy wants us to give up, and he will throw 'rocks' of discouragement and weariness at us to get us to stop walking forward.

Thankfully, Father God will never let us go. He will hold on to us even when we feel we can't hold on. We can rest like a child in His strong arms during those weary times knowing that He will never give up on us.

Always remember this; God does not see you as you see yourself. I have never forgotten an experience I had many years ago when I was emotionally depleted and chronically fatigued. I dragged myself and my children to church "again" and I don't remember what the message was about, but when the invitation to come forward for ministry was given, I began to drag myself to the front of the church "again" for prayer. As I was walking down the aisle, the Pastor, who was very gifted in the prophetic, raised

His arm, pointed at me, and said emphatically, "Mighty woman of God. You are a mighty woman of God"! Looking back, even though I felt weak and needy, I believe that the commendation I was given was in relation to my perseverance. I felt anything but mighty. Sometimes if all we can do is faithfully put one foot after the other, then God is well-pleased with us.

CHAPTER TWENTY

Confession of The Word of God

The word of our testimony, or our confession, is vital in spiritual warfare and transformation.

> Psalm 50:23 says, (KJV) *"Whoso offereth praise glorifieth me: and to him that ordereth **his conversation** aright will I shew the salvation of God".* (emphasis mine)

As we read before in Ephesians 6, the word of God is the offensive weapon of the sword of the Spirit. There is great power in confessing the Word of God. The Bible has much to say about this.

What is the point of proclaiming God's promises and asking Him for an answer to prayer and then going about being negative and confessing that your situation looks hopeless? When we do this, we negate the power of prayer and the promises of God in our situation. Scripture tells us that we will get fruit from our words regardless of whether they are positive or negative. Words spoken over us by others when we were children or at any point in our lives have a powerful effect, either to build us up or destroy us.

Spoken words can be a blessing or a curse and words give access to the enemy not only in our lives but also to those about us. Words will take root in our hearts either to build us up or tear us down. Good words produce good fruit. Bad words produce bad fruit.

> Proverbs 18:21 (KJV) *"Death and life are in the power of the tongue: and they that love it shall eat the fruit thereof"*.

We see in Genesis 1 that God created the world with His words. When He proclaimed, "Let there be light", the light was manifest. Whatever God wanted to come into existence in the creation of the earth came by His command, "Let there be..."

All things were called into being by God's spoken word. We are made in God's image, and we have the same ability to call life into every situation by the Word of God. The primary thing that sets us apart as human beings from the animal kingdom, other than having an eternal spirit, is the power of speech.

When the earth began to be repopulated after the time of the flood, the people of Babylon decided to build a tower that reached the heavens as a monument to themselves. This was an act of independence and self-idolatry where the people were virtually seeking to deify themselves. This lacked the reverence and humility that we, as God's creation should practice.

> Gen. 11:4 (NIV) *"Then they said, "Come, let us build ourselves a city, with a tower that reaches to the heavens, so that we may make a name for ourselves; otherwise we will be scattered over the face of the whole earth."5 But the Lord came down to see the city and the tower the people were building. 6 The Lord said, "If as one people speaking the same language they have begun to do this, then nothing they plan to do will be impossible for them. 7 Come, let us go down and confuse their language so they will not understand each other."*

The people of Babylon were using their words to communicate with each other in this monumental act of pride, so God chose to confuse their language so that they could not fulfill this rebellious act of defiance. Our speech can be used for selfish ambition or to build others up.

> Eph. 4:29 (NIV) *"Do not let any unwholesome talk come out of your mouths, but only what is helpful for building others up according to their needs, that it may benefit those who listen".*

The positive words that we speak when we release them in faith, will give God the opportunity to move on our behalf, but if we speak in agreement with the negative words of the enemy, we give him access to whatever or whoever we are speaking over, whether it's ourselves, our family, others, our church, etc. Words hold the power of life or death in the spirit realm. This is why Jesus said that whatever you bind on earth will be bound in heaven and whatever you loose on earth will be loosed in heaven. Our speech allows us to use our authority in Christ to break off satanic powers from people and situations, and we can also bind people into the healing, restoring power of Christ. However, we need to be aware that even idle words affect everything around us.

> Matthew 12:35-37 (NIV) *"A good man brings good things out of the good stored up in him, and an evil man brings evil things out of the evil stored up in him. 36 But I tell you that everyone will have to give account on the day of judgement for every empty word they have spoken. 37 For by your words you will be acquitted, and by your words you will be condemned."*

This is why we need to take the word of God and confess it over our lives and families when we are seeking victory and deliverance from the hand of the enemy. If we choose to confess the negative things about ourselves, or our children's lives then we are reinforcing these things in the spirit realm. If we choose to release faith in what God is doing in our lives, then the Spirit of God is released to move on our behalf.

Negative, faithless words that come from our sinful, wounded soul, only serve to reinforce the strongholds of the enemy. If we refuse to agree with negative thoughts and feelings and choose to declare who God is to us and His promises for us, we can take ground back from the enemy and make a recovery. This is what the scripture refers to when it says, "We walk by faith and not by sight", (2 Cor. 5:7). An important part of our recovery from past issues is to declare the Word of God over ourselves.

God promised childless Abraham and Sarah that they would be the progenitors of a great nation even though they were old and barren. He changed Abram's name meaning "high father" to "Abraham," "father of a multitude" and his wife's name from "Sarai," "my princess," to "Sarah," "mother of nations" (Genesis 17:15–16). In doing this, God was teaching them to call things that were not yet existent into existence, just as He did in the act of creation of the world and mankind.

Speaking of Abraham, God said in Romans 4: 17(KJV) *"(As it is written, I have made thee a father of many nations,) before him whom he believed, even God, who quickeneth the dead, and **calleth those things which be not as though they were**."* (emphasis mine).

What do you want to exist instead of what you already have? Call it into being according to the promises of God. Call healing and faith into hopeless situations. Call repentance and righteousness into being over your family. Declare God's promises from His Word over every negative situation. Don't speak what you've got, speak what you want and what God says instead. This takes self-control so we must reign our tongue in as it's very easy to speak negatively without thinking.

James 1:26, (AMPC) *"If anyone thinks himself to be religious (piously observant of the external duties of his faith) and does not bridle his tongue but deludes his own heart, this person's religious service is worthless (futile, barren)"*.

This scripture says that you can practice all the spiritual principles that you know, but if you don't control your tongue your religious practices are useless or in vain.

Doing something in Vain – *This is an adjective which means 'not achieving the desired outcome', 'futile', 'unsuccessful', 'lacking substance or worth', 'hollow', and 'fruitless'.* **http://www.future-perfect.co.uk/grammar-tip/is-it-vain-vane-or-vein/**

Jesus said in John 6:63 (KJV) *"It is the spirit that quickeneth; the flesh profiteth nothing: the words that I speak unto you, they are spirit, and they are life"*.

When we speak Christ's words, we bring forth life because His word is empowered by His Spirit".

1 Peter 1:24-25 (KJV) *"For all flesh is as grass, and all the glory of man as the flower of grass. The grass withereth, and the flower thereof falleth away:*
25 But the word of the Lord endureth for ever. And this is the word which by the gospel is preached unto you".

Christ was the Word of God made manifest in the flesh (John 1:14) and if we are followers of Him, we must speak things that are in alignment with His words and not from our fleshly reactions or feelings, particularly when we are in the middle of a battle.

God wants us to be careful with our speech. James 1:19 (NIV) *"My dear brothers and sisters, take note of this: Everyone should be quick to listen, slow to speak and slow to become angry..."*

James 3:5 (NIV) *"Likewise, the tongue is a small part of the body, but it makes great boasts. Consider what a great forest is set on fire by a small spark."*

A small word of gossip can start a chain reaction just like a spark can create a huge forest fire. Look at how the media manipulates information these days and creates great controversy through gossip, innuendo, and speculation. Words are powerful and we must guard the words of our mouths and bring them into alignment with the Word of God.

CHAPTER TWENTY-ONE

The Religious Spirit

A major deception that allows Satan to bring people into bond-age is having a "religious spirit". True Christianity is not and never has been, just another religion. In fact, it is not a religion at all. Unfortunately, man will take a gift from God and then put his own 'spin' on it until centuries later the gift has become completely restructured. A bit like Chinese whispers. You start off telling some-one a message then they pass it on to someone else, then they tell someone else, and so on, until centuries later it is distorted beyond recognition.

Christ came to the world as the "Word of God" made manifest in the flesh to show the heart of God as opposed to those who prac-ticed many religions. He declared that He was "the way, the truth, and the life". The Pharisees who were the religious leaders in Israel at the time of Christ, gradually changed Judaism from a religion of love, relationship, and sacrifice to one of religious legalism.

In Matthew 23:13–15 *"Jesus pronounced a series of stern warnings against Pharisaism, a danger to today's spiritual leaders just as it was in ancient times. Jesus condemned the Jewish religious teachers of His day, saying, "Woe to you,*

*scribes and Pharisees, hypocrites! For you devour widows'
houses, and for a pretense make long prayers. Therefore
you will receive greater condemnation".* **https://www.
gotquestions.org/devour-widows-houses.html**

Christ made a distinction between all the false concepts of religion and what it means to come into a relationship with God as our
Father. Christ presented to us God's desire for "sons" who would
become a new creation, a habitation of God. When Christianity is
practiced as a religion it is an extremely hard, legalistic taskmaster
because people come back under the law instead of grace.

Today, a religious spirit is a satanic counterfeit of true Godliness.
It runs in parallel with God's word, but this spirit is not gracious,
loving, and merciful but rather rigid and performance driven. This
type of approach quenches much of our natural God-given human
traits because we are trying to control ourselves by our own flesh,
or strength. This cannot produce the Godly fruit of the Spirit in
a person's life because it does not originate from God Himself.
This is a distortion of the gospel. Truth, when taken out of context,
becomes error.

The religious spirit denies the need for the power of God in our
lives by working solely from our own strength. This becomes a
very heavy yoke to bear.

2 Timothy 3:5 *"... having a form of godliness but denying
its power. Have nothing to do with such people".*

Religion is a belief system that requires adherence to its laws
and regulations from its followers in order to appease some deity.
This type of thinking then leads to a sense of impending punishment or displeasure from that deity when we fail to reach those
standards. This type of structure was the basis of the Old Testament
pattern. The only way that the people could be forgiven was to

have the blood sacrifice of an animal offered up by the priesthood on their behalf as atonement for their sins.

However, God devised a plan to bring us back into a relationship with Himself through the death and resurrection of Christ, who was the ultimate offering for sin, once and for all. When we receive this gift of Christ's sacrifice, we also receive the indwelling presence of the Spirit of God. His Spirit gives us a new set of values and helps to transform us from the inside out while providing unconditional love to us as we are in the process of change.

Romans 1:16 *"For I am not ashamed of the gospel, because it is the <u>power</u> of God that brings salvation to everyone who believes: first to the Jew, then to the Gentile"*.

Sometimes, people think that if they start attending a church and reading their Bible that they have become Christians. Some also take it for granted that if their family went to church and they also have continued to go to church regularly as well, that they are Christians. But as previously mentioned in this book, it is only when we make a conscious choice to receive Christ as Saviour, and His Spirit becomes reinstated within our hearts that we are truly born again into God's kingdom. You may have heard the saying that sitting in a garage every Sunday doesn't make you a car, any more than sitting in church every Sunday makes you a Christian.

A religious spirit can frequently be passed on to us and be modelled behaviorally to us by our forebears. A person who is born again may start attending a church where there is a religious spirit and because of immaturity may not be able to discern it. The influence of this spirit will remain with us until we discern it and break all agreement with it and its deception by the authority of Christ. We will then need to renew our minds over time so that we can be released from all the false concepts that have formed within us because of this spirit.

This performance-based religion keeps us from coming into a deep, loving relationship with God. Speaking of the New Covenant that was to come, the prophet Hosea indicated that there would come a time when there would be a new, intimate relationship available to man with God.

> Hosea 2:16 (NIV) *"In that day," declares the LORD, "you will call me 'my husband'; you will no longer call me 'my master.'*

People under the influence of a legalistic spirit can be 'driven' by continually feeling that they must perform to be acceptable to God and others. It produces a concept of a God, who is never fully satisfied with them. It is frequently accompanied by a legalistic, judgmental, critical, self-righteous spirit. Oftentimes, people operating under this spirit lack peace and they can frequently experience anxiety because they never feel that they have done enough to be acceptable to God or conversely, they can become very self-righteous.

> Luke 18:10-15 (NIV) *10 "Two men went up to the temple to pray, one a Pharisee and the other a tax collector. 11 The Pharisee stood by himself and prayed: 'God, I thank you that I am not like other people—robbers, evildoers, adulterers—or even like this tax collector. 12 I fast twice a week and give a tenth of all I get.' 13 "But the tax collector stood at a distance. He would not even look up to heaven, but beat his breast and said, 'God, have mercy on me, a sinner.' 14 "I tell you that this man, rather than the other, went home justified before God. For all those who exalt themselves will be humbled, and those who humble themselves will be exalted."*

A person with a religious spirit can be more interested in their position in the church, (like the Pharisees) than in their relationship with God. Often, they will only want to connect with people in relation to some form of Christian ministry rather than being genuinely interested in a personal relationship with them. Many such people will be dogmatically committed to a specific denomination more than they are to Christ Himself.

Just as the Pharisees criticized and tried to undermine Jesus, the religious spirit will judge and criticize any new move of God and the people who are operating within it. It will always work out of the religious traditions of men instead of the Word of God.

> Mark 7:7-9 (KJV) *"Howbeit in vain do they worship me, teaching for doctrines the commandments of men. For laying aside the commandment of God, ye hold the tradition of men, as the washing of pots and cups: and many other such like things ye do. And he said unto them, Full well ye reject the commandment of God, that ye may keep your own tradition"*.

Christ said in Matthew 4:4 (KJV) *"...It is written, Man shall not live by bread alone, **but by every word** that proceedeth out of the mouth of God"*. (Emphasis mine)

Any doctrine or church practices that have no foundation in the word of God are always based upon religious traditions. For instance, in the Old Testament, the High Priest's role was to offer up the blood of sacrificial animals as a sin offering for the people. He alone had the authority to pass through a veil into the Holy of Holies to perform this task.

Hebrews 9:13 (NIV) *13 "The blood of goats and bulls and the ashes of a heifer sprinkled on those who are ceremonially unclean sanctify them so that they are outwardly clean.*

14 How much more, then, will the blood of Christ, who through the eternal Spirit offered himself unblemished to God, cleanse our consciences from acts that lead to death, so that we may serve the living God!

15 For this reason Christ is the mediator of a new covenant, that those who are called may receive the promised eternal inheritance—now that he has died as a ransom to set them free from the sins committed under the first covenant".

Christ was the final offering for sin. He is now the High Priest of our confession.

Hebrews 3:1 (NIV) *"Therefore, holy brothers and sisters, who share in the heavenly calling, fix your thoughts on Jesus, whom we acknowledge as our apostle and **high priest**".*

Christ entered through the veil by His own personal sacrifice. When He cried, "It is finished", upon the cross, scripture tells us that the veil in the temple separating people from the Holy Place was rent from top to bottom signifying no more separation from God. It also meant that there was no further need for blood sacrifice or burnt offerings so therefore the priestly pattern from the Old Testament was completed.

The New Testament pattern for the church is outlined for us in Hebrews 4:11-13. (KJV)

11 "And he gave some, apostles; and some, prophets; and some, evangelists; and some, pastors and teachers;

12 For the perfecting of the saints, for the work of the ministry, for the edifying of the body of Christ:

13 Till we all come in the unity of the faith, and of the knowledge of the Son of God, unto a perfect man, unto the measure of the stature of the fullness of Christ:"

We no longer require a human being as a mediator between God and ourselves because Timothy 2:5 says *"For there is one God and one mediator between God and mankind, the man Christ Jesus..."*

Because the religious spirit is a counterfeit of the Spirit of Christ, it works on external rules and observances to be made right or justified with God but only the blood of Christ can do that. The Old Testament promoted a legalistic system that did nothing to change the hearts of men.

Galatians 2:16 (NIV) *"...know that a person is not justified by the works of the law, but by faith in Jesus Christ. So, we too have put our faith in Christ Jesus that we may be justified by faith in Christ and not by the works of the law, because by the works of the law no one will be justified."*

A person or a denomination with a religious spirit, will often 'camp' on a move of God from way back in the past and yet be unwilling to acknowledge or accept a current fresh move of the Spirit of God. Scripture says that in the last days, God will pour out His Spirit on all flesh. It says that our sons and daughters will prophecy, young men shall see visions, and old men shall dream dreams (Joel 2:28). Many churches have embraced the current movement of the Holy Spirit, but some have not.

The religious leaders in Jesus' day were the ones who had him crucified because he challenged them on their practices and religious traditions, and He exposed the condition of their hearts. They were full of law but lacked love and compassion for others.

Luke 20:46-47 (NIV) *"Beware of the teachers of the law. They like to walk around in flowing robes and love to be greeted with respect in the marketplaces and have the most important seats in the synagogues and the places of honor at banquets. 47 They devour widows' houses and for a show make lengthy prayers. These men will be punished most severely".*

Judgemental Spirit

A judgemental spirit will bring bondage into our lives because we always reap what we sow. If we make a judgement about someone else, it is quite common for that thing that we have judged to become something that we will wrestle with ourselves. A pastor that I know went through burnout in his younger years and it took some time to recover. I remember his wife telling me how, at that time, two other pastors judged him in relation to this. Then some years later, both of those pastors also experienced burnout themselves.

Joyce Meyer speaks about this too, when she tells of how she experienced morning sickness in one of her pregnancies. She had never had a problem with this in her prior pregnancies, but the Lord showed her an instance when she judged a pregnant lady for 'not pushing through' and getting into church attendance because she was experiencing morning sickness at that time. She went on to say that she had to repent of this judgement that she had 'sown' towards that lady.

If you can identify with any of this, then you need to repent and renounce all agreement with this spirit to break free from anything that you have sown. If you have not already done so, ask Christ to come and dwell within your heart. You need to break all soul ties with that religious spirit and any organization or people that you have associated with who operate in this spirit. Again, this doesn't mean that you necessarily break all connections to people, especially if they are family, but you must be led by God in choosing your affiliations.

If you recognize this as a generational spirit, you need to repent on behalf of your ancestors as well and forgive them for passing this on to you. Then ask God to forgive you and your ancestors and to cleanse your bloodline and the family DNA with the blood of Christ. If you have offspring, you will need to include them in this prayer for forgiveness asking the blood of Christ to cleanse them and your bloodline and to break the power of this spirit from them.

CHAPTER TWENTY-TWO

Generational Curses

O ver the years when speaking about generational curses, I have heard many Christians say, ''I thought that this was all dealt with at the cross". We all believe that Christ dealt with sin and sickness and curses at the cross, but does that mean that we never have to deal with sin or sickness after salvation? We all know that we do. As mentioned earlier, there is a battle for the fruits of our salvation inheritance that must be possessed by faith and there are 'giants' that must be dispossessed before this can happen. It is no different when dealing with generational curses. It takes the discernment of the Spirit, and keys of the kingdom, to recognize and deal with generational curses.

While the power of the cross has dealt with generational curses as well as sin and sickness, as Christians we must enforce that power over every obstacle that is inherent to us as individuals. Satan is a usurper, and he will attempt to take the ground that is not legally his if we allow him to do so.

Ezekiel 18:1-4 (NIV) *"The word of the Lord came to me: 2 What do you people mean by quoting this proverb about the land of Israel: The parents eat sour grapes, and the children's teeth are set on edge'? 3 As surely as I live, declares the Sovereign Lord, you will no longer quote this proverb in Israel. 4 For everyone belongs to me, the parent as well as the child—both alike belong to me. The one who sins is the one who will die."*

I believe that this scripture is saying that there will come a point in time when generational curses will be dealt with (by the redemptive power of the cross) and that children will no longer have to live with the bitter consequences of their father's sins. Christ dealt with all sin, sickness, and demonic oppression through the power of His death and resurrection. We, as Christians, have the authority to put off the old life and put on the new. Though we may inherit 'sour grapes' from our ancestors, the power of the cross gives us the means to overcome that poor inheritance.

There are numerous generational curses that can be passed on to us. This is why we must discern whether the issues that we are battling with now, are something that was initiated within our own lifetime or if they come from a 'door' that was left open by an ancestor.

Sins that can pass on generationally can include incest, sexual deviation, the spirit of rejection, addictive behaviour, adultery, pride, orphan spirit, greed, violence, idolatry, false religious practices, dishonesty, thieving, occult practices plus many more.

Occult practices such as witchcraft, contacting the dead, consorting with spirits or fortune telling, using a Ouija board, etc. all open a door to the demonic realm. This open door can lead to a person experiencing mental illness, and all sorts of oppression. I have met a couple of Christians who could see into the demonic realm around them, and this can be very frightening and tormenting for those who experience it. Doors left open by occult practices from our forebears can usher in a spirit of deception that leaves future

generations susceptible to being drawn into ungodly spiritual practices and torment.

We all have natural and spiritual gifts that are meant to be
anointed and empowered by the Spirit of God within us. When
a person has been involved in the occult or has an ancestral door
open to the occult realm this can bring confusion to a person's
spiritual gifts even after salvation. At times, he or she might operate in a spirit of prophecy or word of knowledge that comes from
their God-given gift by the Spirit of God. At other times they could
receive revelation from an unclean spirit and not even be aware of
it. So even after becoming a Christian, people can 'double stream'
prophetically, one moment hearing the voice of the Spirit of God
and the next picking up on a spirit of deception. It is not that these
things weren't dealt with at the cross of Christ but until we recognize them, we won't be able to deal with them effectively.

Sometimes a susceptibility to listening to the wrong voices can
come from familiar spirits that prior ancestors have affiliated with
through fortune telling or other occult practices.

There have been many revelations released to the body of Christ
in the last few years in relation to breaking generational curses. I
believe that when the door to iniquitous spirits has been opened
through ungodly practices, vows, or ungodly covenants made by
our ancestors, we can be influenced by the "familiar" (family)
spirits that our ancestors have associated with, and consequently
inherit bloodline curses through our DNA.

Curses can be passed on generationally through idolatry or
worship of foreign gods.

Exodus 20:5 (NIV) *"You shall not bow down to them or
worship them; for I, the LORD your God, am a jealous
God, punishing the children for the sin of the parents to the
third and fourth generation of those who hate me"*.

Numbers 14:18 (NIV) *"The Lord is slow to anger, abounding in love and forgiving sin and rebellion. Yet he does not leave the guilty unpunished; he punishes the children for the sin of the parents to the third and fourth generation".*

Spirit of Pharmakeia

Certain groups or cultures, especially those in the East, have used drugs or potions to bypass the natural senses to open spiritual portals while seeking revelation from the spirit world. In doing this they expose themselves to demonic spirits and these iniquitous practices can leave future generations open to oppression.

"There are gateways or portals down to the pit and out into the universe in either case to contact beings from other dimensions. There are good and evil portals. YHVH revealed to Jacob a good portal or gateway to heaven at the site of the future Temple Mount when he dreamed of the ladder to heaven. Yeshua is the gateway or doorway to the Father in heaven (John 1:51). But there are evil gateways that men open up illicitly through pharmakeia or drug induced states.

Revelation 9:21, Sorceries. Gr. pharmakeia. Pharmakeia is a methodology to circumvent Elohim and to open the doorways into the supernatural. It is the mix of science along with magical arts, occultic or hidden, demonic, angelic or paranormal realm and medicine, potions, or herbs for sorcerous reasons to open the mind so you can put yourself in contact with what is beyond the gate or the boundaries YHVH has established between the natural and supernatural (including the demonic) realm". **https://hoshanarabbah. org/blog/2016/10/08/what-is-pharmakeia/**

190

If the Holy Spirit reveals a 'door' to the unclean spirit world that was opened by our ancestors, we need to deal with it by repenting for our antecedent's participation in the occult or iniquitous practices, as well as our own, if necessary, before breaking the soul ties with those ancestors, living or dead. We also need to break the soul ties to the spirits that they have affiliated with.

Dealing with other generational open doors that bring spiritual oppression

Many times, we can see where certain personality traits, such as stubbornness or rebellion for example, have been passed on to us by preceding generations.

> 1 Samuel 15:23 (KJV) *"For rebellion is as the sin of witchcraft, and stubbornness is as iniquity and idolatry."*

There has been much new revelation and teaching about bringing generational sin to God as the judge in the courts of heaven. Pastor Robert Henderson has a book called "Operating in the Courts of Heaven", which I highly recommend. He teaches that there are times when, in bringing our requests and petitions before God, that we can approach Him either as Father (Luke 11:5-8), Friend (Luke 11:11-13), or as Judge (Luke 18:1-7). So, when dealing with the iniquities of our forebears who gave the enemy a legal right to afflict and oppress them and their offspring, we need to approach God as Judge.

Because generational curses have familiar spirits attached to them, I personally prefer to deal with them through God's courtroom and ask Him to judge the spirit that is attached to our family bloodline. When we have been born again, Satan does not have the legal right to maintain generational strongholds over us. Therefore, we can repent of our ancestors' sins and forgive them for opening the door to the enemy and petition God to judge and sentence our enemy and evict them from those places where he trespassed on our ground. We can also petition Him to restore what was stolen as this is scriptural. (Joel 2)

Satan is the accuser (Greek word **antidikos**) of the brethren (Rev. 12:10). **Strongs Concordance: antidikos: an opponent, adversary. Usage: an opponent (at law), an adversary.**

This is a general outline for breaking generational curses

God keeps records of many things as well as our family history (Revelation 20:12). In approaching God, we are asking Him to review the records of our ancestral history and to reveal to us any outstanding iniquity that needs to be dealt with. Whatever our ancestors have repented of and dealt with by the power of the cross, should no longer affect us.

We ask Him to summon to the courtroom any ungodly spirits that have gained a legal right to our bloodline through ancestral sin so that they may be judged by Him.

Our only claim to right standing and victory in the courtroom is because of the blood of Christ, the cross of Calvary, and His victory over every demon, sin, and sickness.

We need to confess our ancestors' sins as God reveals them to us, plus our own if we have continued to practice these things. Sometimes, we are aware of what those specific sins were, but if not, we can repent for inherent sins known and unknown.

We then forgive those ancestors for passing this curse on to us. We ask God to forgive and cleanse the bloodline and the very DNA of our family with the blood of Christ, going right back to Adam and Eve. If we or the person we are praying for have offspring we can also ask Him to release the cleansing power of His blood over them and to break soul ties with our ungodly ancestors, ungodly spirits, and practices.

We petition God to make a judgement on our behalf that He would award in our family records that this has been 'PAID FOR IN FULL' by the blood of Christ. We then ask Him to render a verdict of judgement against the enemy, that every assignment against us must be cancelled, and that he must be evicted from our ground. We declare that the cross of Christ is planted firmly behind us and our family thereby cancelling all legal rights of the enemy to have access to our family and future offspring. We can then request that God would graciously award to us restitution of all that has been stolen from us (Joel 2:25).

This is an outline of how to pray but it is not necessary to use a rigid formula. We may not always get a revelation of where or how a particular family curse came into our bloodline, but we can still repent for our ancestors and our own iniquity that allowed a curse, or stronghold into the family bloodline and where we have allowed it to be perpetuated.

Christ has cancelled every debt that was held against us, but as the enemy is a usurper who will try to hold on to that which does not legally belong to him, we must exercise our authority and legal rights when he trespasses upon our ground. We can use verse 14 from Colossians 2 as a "sword" to cut off and dispossess his hold upon our family.

Colossians 2:13 *"When you were dead in your trespasses and in the uncircumcision of your sinful nature, God made you alive with Christ. He forgave us all our trespasses,* **14 having canceled the debt ascribed to us in the decrees that stood against us. He took it away, nailing it to the cross!** *15 And having disarmed the powers and authorities, He made a public spectacle of them, triumphing over them by the cross".*

Cultural Curses

When we are dealing with curses that come from different cultural backgrounds, we need to assess the spiritual practices and belief systems that our ancestors followed. For example, some cultures practice ancestral worship which is a form of idolatry.

"What does the Bible say about ancestor worship? First, the Bible tells us that the spirits of the dead go to either heaven or hell and do not remain in the natural world (Luke 16:20-31; 2 Corinthians 5:6-10; Hebrews 9:27; Revelation 20:11-15). The belief that spirits continue to reside on earth after death and influence the lives of others is not scriptural.

Second, nowhere in the Bible are we told that the dead act as intermediaries between God and man. But we are told that Jesus Christ was given that role. He was born, lived a sinless life, was crucified for our sins, buried in a grave, resurrected by God, seen by a multitude of witnesses, ascended into heaven, and sits now at the right hand of the Father where He intercedes on the behalf of those who have placed their faith and trust in Him (Acts 26:23; Romans 1:2-5; Hebrews 4:15; 1 Peter 1:3-4). There is only one Mediator between God and man, and that is God's Son, Jesus Christ (1 Timothy 2:5-6; Hebrews 8:6, 9:15, 12:24). Only Christ can fill that role". **https://www. gotquestions.org/ancestor-worship.html**

New age practices – False religions

Throughout history, every culture, regardless of how advanced or primitive it may be, has had a system of law within its society. This structure always includes lawmakers, law enforcers, and those who act in a judicial capacity to determine where the law has been broken and to apply a legal penalty appropriate to the offence.

Every human being has within them an innate sense of the need for justice. If someone cheated us out of our life savings or murdered a loved one, we would want justice. It is the same with God.

If we as human beings were holy, or perfect, we would not have the need for a redeemer or savior. We would not have any crimes or wars if we were perfect. Because of our sinful state, we deserve a penalty imposed upon us for our "crimes" before God.

As God is Holy, only the righteous may enter His presence and dwell with Him eternally. Scripture tells us in Romans 6:23 that the wage (or penalty) of sin is death, but the free gift of righteousness standing with God, and eternal life comes from Christ who took the penalty of sin for us. God imputes righteousness to those who receive Christ so that we can be connected to Him and boldly come to God's throne of grace to receive mercy (Heb. 4:16).

God required justice for mankind's rebellion against Him and for all the hurt and human pain that this rebellion caused.

Christ chose to pay the price for us to have access to the Father and to be acceptable by Him, by shedding His blood for us upon the cross.

Hebrews 9:22 (NLT) *"In fact, according to the law of Moses, nearly everything was purified with blood. For without the shedding of blood, there is no forgiveness".*

This is why Jesus said, *'I am the way and the truth and the life. No one comes to the Father except through me.'* John 14:6 (NIV) It is only because Jesus came to take our punishment and to shed His blood for us, that we can gain access to the Father without guilt or condemnation.

Christ is with God and is God in the mystery of the Holy Trinity, and He is enthroned in power and glory, strength and might. He left His Kingly residence and divine God-head status and powers behind to come to earth as a frail human being. He knew what it was to be rejected by others and scripture says that He suffered all the same temptations that human beings suffer without sinning. He (God) humbled Himself to allow Himself to be tried by His own creation and, to be whipped and crucified by brutal Roman soldiers. He took upon Himself a position of shame as He identified with our sins and was judged by his own creation. If He had been an ordinary, sinful man, He would have just taken the punishment that He deserved, but He was the pure sinless, sacrificial Lamb who willingly gave His life, taking our punishment for sin in our stead. The weight of the sin and suffering that He bore for us upon the cross is beyond our human understanding, but clearly, He bore much more than physical suffering.

> Hebrews 12:2 (NIV) *". . . fixing our eyes on Jesus, the pioneer and perfecter of faith. For the joy set before him he endured the cross, scorning its shame, and sat down at the right hand of the throne of God".*

This magnanimous act of our Creator is singularly the most amazing event that has ever occurred throughout the history of mankind, even dividing man's timeline by the definition of BC and AD (*although secular authorities have redefined its meaning*). If God chose to leave the portals of heaven to create a 'way' back to Himself, then He will not support another path of man's choosing to be reconciled to Him.

> John 10:1 (NIV) *"Very truly I tell you Pharisees, anyone who does not enter the sheep pen by the gate, but climbs in by some other way, is a thief and a robber".*

Jesus came to show us 'the way' in our natural lives and in the spirit realm. His 'word', His 'truth', is the divine path to the spirit realm and He does not amalgamate with others. This is not

Christian dogmatism. Christ Himself is dogmatic in relation to truth and Who He is. If you want to amalgamate Jesus with other spirits or religions, He refuses to comply. There are a multitude of spiritual experiences out there but without Christ and His words, we are wandering around the spirit realm without direction. The Bible is the **Word** of God our 'guide to life and the spirit realm'. Christ was the **Word** made manifest in the flesh.

> John 1:1 (NIV) says, *"In the beginning was the **Word**, and the **Word** was with God, and the **Word** was God".*

Then John goes on to say in verse 14 of chapter 1:

> *"The **Word** became flesh and made His dwelling among us. We have seen His glory, the glory of the one and only Son from the Father, full of **grace** and "**truth**".* (emphasis mine).

Jesus was God's Word, or 'email' sent to us, in the flesh, to give us a direction in the spirit realm. He claimed that He was the **only** way to the Father and that any other way was counterfeit.

When we seek truth through other spiritual channels, we open ourselves to deception. Most people would acknowledge that there is both good and bad in the spirit realm. For instance, some years ago there was a case on the news where a woman and her brother were into some form of witchcraft, and they practiced satanic sexual rites on the woman's twelve-year-old daughter. The daughter became pregnant by her uncle through this, so the couple aborted the fetus and forced her to eat it as part of another satanic ritual. Somehow, this came to the attention of the media and the authorities, and the girl was removed from their influence.

The majority of people would look at this and think that this is disgusting and evil. We would not agree with these practices or with the spirit realm that they were operating in. This is because generally most people have a good sense of right and wrong and can discern what is unhealthy and what is perverted. So normally there would only be a small percentage of society that would be emotionally and psychologically preconditioned and damaged enough to want to participate in such spiritual practices. However, evil does not just want to be acceptable to dysfunctional, marginalized people, but to all people. In order to deceive those who have a better conscience and moral code, darkness must present itself as light. Evil must create a counterfeit that seems acceptable and appealing.

Counterfeit: made in imitation of something else with intent to deceive
https://www.merriam-webster.com/dictionary/counterfeit

One of the 'traps' that people fall into is in feeling that they are being magnanimous in being all-embracing of all faiths. Sometimes, this magnanimity is just another form of pride that says, "I'm all-encompassing, generous, and inclusive". This is a spirit that is invading society today. We **should** always love **people** unconditionally but that does not mean we validate **practices** that are forbidden by God, the King of Heaven.

As Christians, we are to respect and love all others regardless of their faith, practices, or belief system. It is not our place to judge or condemn other people groups. Christians who do this are operating under the religious spirit that I have previously mentioned. Neither is it our place to coerce people into the kingdom of God as that is a violation of their free will. Scripture says that it is the kindness of God that leads us to salvation (Romans 2:3-4). As much as God wants all people to be saved, He will not violate their free will if they wish to remain in darkness.

However, if we fellowship with darkness in our current lives, we will end up in eternal darkness in our afterlife.

2 Corinthians 11:14-15 (NIV) *"And no wonder, for Satan himself masquerades as an angel of light. 15 It is not surprising, then, if his servants also masquerade as servants of righteousness. Their end will be what their actions deserve."*

We can't choose our own way of salvation.

Proverbs 14:12 (KJV) says, *"There is a way which seemeth right unto a man, but the end thereof are the ways of death"*.

There is always a spirit behind every spiritual pathway that we choose, so we must be wise and follow the pathway of the Saviour and Shepherd, Jesus Christ. The Holy Spirit is the only Spirit from God.

Romans 8:14 (KJV) *"For as many as are led by the Spirit of God, they are sons of God."*

If the spirit that you are following is not in agreement with the Word of God or producing the fruit of the Spirit of God, then it is false, because all scripture was inspired and preserved by the Holy Spirit. God does not contradict Himself or violate His own word to suit a person's circumstances.

If we have participated in 'new age' practices before coming to Christ or have ancestors who have practiced these things, we need to repent and renounce these things and break off soul ties to the spirits and to the people who have practiced them. The Bible speaks about two kingdoms, the kingdom of light and the kingdom of darkness. Jesus came to open the 'way', legally for man to have access to the kingdom of light through His death and resurrection.

John 10:1–3 (NIV) *1 "Very truly I tell you Pharisees, anyone who does not enter the sheep pen by the gate, but climbs in by some other way, is a thief and a robber. 2 The one who enters by the gate is the shepherd of the sheep. 3 The gatekeeper opens the gate for him, and the sheep listen to his voice".*

The choice is ours. Do we follow Jesus Christ, or do we make up our own way? The choice is ours as individuals who have free will. We must receive and follow Christ, regardless of our personal desires or cultural background.

Recently, I prayed for an Australian Indigenous man, and I felt in the Spirit that there was a place where cursing and pointing the bone at someone had been practiced by an ancestor. I led the man in prayer to renounce and repent of this sin in his bloodline and to apply the blood of Christ to this generational iniquity. After prayer, the man confirmed that this was 'spot on' and that one of his ancestors was a shaman in his tribe who frequently practiced these things. This type of practice involves invoking a spirit that is not from God to harm others and operating in this spirit is a type of witchcraft. Spirits reign over tribes and nations. Therefore, we need to break any negative, generational, and cultural ties with ancestral spirits as well as personal soul ties to practices and people from our past, again this does not mean all relational soul ties to our forebears, only the negative ones.

CHAPTER TWENTY-THREE

Historic Trauma Response

Trauma can be passed down not only through an individual's bloodline but through cultural groups as well. If a major traumatic occurrence has impacted a people group permanently, thereby altering their identity and lifestyle, this can influence many generations to come. This happens when a people group has been overtaken by another race of people or dispossessed from their native homeland. Historic Trauma Response involves the emotional, spiritual, and social repercussions upon a race of people where they have been marginalized, displaced, enslaved, abused, and diminished as a culture. This creates despondency and a victim mentality, and this disconnect leads to a diminution of identity and purpose. The loss of their old traditions and lifestyle plus the inability to fully integrate with the new culture can leave a cultural group feeling that they are in 'no man's land'. This loss of identity in turn makes them vulnerable to a spirit of apathy and addiction. Statistically, for generations later, alcoholism, drug, and sexual abuse are many times greater than is found in mainstream society.

"Historical trauma (HT) is cumulative emotional and psychological wounding over the lifespan and across

generations, emanating from massive group trauma experiences; the historical trauma response (HTR) is the constellation of features in reaction to this trauma. The HTR often includes depression, self-destructive behavior, suicidal thoughts and gestures, anxiety, low self-esteem, anger, and difficulty recognizing and expressing emotions. It may include substance abuse, often an attempt to avoid painful feelings through self-medication. Historical unre-solved grief is the associated effect that accompanies HTR; this grief may be considered fixated, impaired, delayed, and/or disenfranchised". **https://www.tandfonline.com/doi/abs/10.1080/02791072.2003.10399988**

For many of our indigenous people in Australia, there has been a heritage of being displaced, diminished, and disempowered and consequently, this has led to a loss of identity, and significance. While our government has made some effort to recompense our native people for past wrongs, there is still a deep wounding generationally that I believe needs to be addressed spiritually.

Many of them still have tribal spirits operating over them that are not from God. The spirit of desolation and captivity, which comes from wounds within their soul realm, leaves them vulnerable to addictive and abusive behavior. The following are some statistics that relate to these issues.

The prevalence of family violence and child abuse in Aboriginal communities – https://aifs.gov.au/cfca/publications/child-abuse-and-family-violence-aboriginal-communities/prevalence-family-violence-and child abuse

"Accurate statistics about the incidence of family violence in Aboriginal communities are scarce (Bolger 1991). Although the statistics that are available are imperfect, 'they are sufficient to

demonstrate that the occurrence of violence in Indigenous com-munities and among Indigenous people 'is disproportionately high in comparison to the rates of the same types of violence in the Australian population as a whole' (Memmott, Stacy, Chambers & Keys 2001: 6). O'Donoghue (2001) illustrates the extent of the problem of family violence, noting that many Indigenous children are growing up in communities where violence has become 'a nor-mal and ordinary part of life' (O'Donoghue 2001: 15).

Ferrante and colleagues (1996) suggest that Aboriginal women living in rural and remote areas are one and a half times more likely to be a victim of domestic violence than those living in met-ropolitan areas and 45 times more likely to be a victim of domestic violence than non-Aboriginal women.

While there are few figures available from Western Australia, available data from the Northern Territory indicate that there are around 6,000 incidents of assault on Indigenous women in the Northern Territory per year. That is, approximately one-third of the Northern Territory's Indigenous female population is assaulted each year. Weapons are reported to be used in around 50-60% of Indigenous attacks between spouses (Memmott et al. 2001

CHILD ABUSE – There is little information available on the prevalence of child abuse in Australia generally, or for Aboriginal and Torres Strait Islander children specifically. The most reliable statistics available are the national child protection statistics that have been collated by the Australian Institute of Health and Welfare (AIHW) since 1990. These statistics suggest that the number of child protection notifications in Australia is increasing every year, with 115,471 notifications being made in 2000/01, 27,367 of these being cases substantiated or confirmed as child abuse (AIHW 2000/01). The statistics also reveal that Aboriginal and Torres Strait Islander children are significantly over-represented in the protection and care system of all states and territories (AIHW 2000/01). This trend has been evident each year since the first collation in 1990."

https://aifs.gov.au/cfca/publications/child-abuse-and-family-vio-lence-aboriginal-communities/prevalence-family-violence-and child abuse

Recently, there have been several reported deaths of our indigenous babies who were born with syphilis and consequently passed away.

"There is an ongoing outbreak of infectious syphilis affecting young Aboriginal and Torres Strait Islander people, predominately aged between 15 and 29 years, living in northern Australia.

The outbreak began in northern Queensland in January 2011, extended to the Northern Territory in July 2013, and then onto the Kimberley region of Western Australia in June 2014. In March 2017, South Australia declared an outbreak in the Western, Eyre, and Far North regions from November 2016

However, it must be noted that the AIHW statistics only deal with cases of child abuse which were reported to authorities and are an underestimate of the incidence of child abuse across the nation. There is a 'flaw in the current statistics regarding child abuse or child sexual abuse, due to the [perceived] lack of response when cases are reported. Many Aboriginal women believe that "it is no use reporting because they don't believe you anyway' (Robertson 2000: 100)." **http://www.health.gov.au/internet/main/publishing. nsf/Content/ohp-infectious-syphilis-outbreak.htm**

The first point of all restoration for any individual no matter what their culture is receiving Christ as Saviour. He is not the "white man's God", He is the Saviour of the entire World who came to the Jewish people first and then to all mankind. Once we receive the Spirit of Adoption and the forgiveness of God for ourselves, we are then able to move to the place where we are no longer orphans or 'victims who were dispossessed' but people who have come into a new kingdom with God as our Father and we learn to receive all the rights, privileges, and responsibilities of being a child of God. Unless we have come to the place of a new identity and inheritance, we will never be able to be free from the grief, violation, and loss of the past.

In dealing with Historic Trauma, (whatever our background) we must deal with all the negative things that have impacted our people group. Those things that were inherited in the natural as well as in the spirit. Grief, trauma, rejection, and negative, prejudicial, sinful responses can be passed on to successive generations. Ancient trauma can include; tremendous anger, resentment, bitterness and frustration, hopelessness, and despair. Once we are born again, these things have no legal right to oppress us anymore, but they can remain if we do not know our legal rights and enforce that defeat. Remember Joshua and the children of Israel had to evict the "giants" before they could possess the Promised Land.

I believe that the best approach to Historic trauma is to take the enemy to the court of heaven and to approach God as Judge. As we are redeemed, blood-bought people of God the enemy has no legal right to oppress us or our offspring anymore, but as our ancestors allowed these spirits to remain, they will keep us in patterns of bondage and pain until we deal with them.

We have been given a new inheritance which we did not earn but was given to us by the Grace of God through the blood of our sacrifice, Jesus. We do not stand on our own rights but upon the purchase price of the blood of the Lamb of God. God did not pay that high price to redeem us from the enemy to have us live under the dominion of the enemy's yoke.

Personally, I would pray like this, but this is only an outline. I ask Father God if I may approach Him as Judge and that He would hear my confession, and my charges against the enemy and see the wounds of the past that are affecting me and my family. I would acknowledge that historic trauma has been passed on to me and my offspring through my forebears. I would name the people group/s who dispossessed my people and say, "Father, you know how they treated my people, You saw it all. You saw their arrogance and pride as they treated us as an inferior race. You saw our rights; our freedom being taken away and the abuse of our ancestors by them. You saw that we were herded up like cattle and displaced from our homeland. You saw where we were forced into servitude. You know the violation and trauma that this has produced and the displacement of belonging, loss of identity and loss of purpose, the confusion. You know where our land was stolen from us. You know where we do not fully relate to our past and where we have been unable to integrate fully into a new culture. We sometimes feel that we are in "no man's land". We feel like orphans and castoffs. You also see where we, in turn, have become abusers and have taken on a victim mentality. You know the curse that has come upon us of addictive behavior, relational breakdowns, domestic violence, sexual abuse, and purposelessness. You see the desolation of our children's inheritance. *(Not all of this will relate to you personally but check the list below and apply and add anything that does relate to you).*

I choose to forgive the individuals and the people group who displaced us, abused us, and violated our rights. I ask you to forgive us for our anger, blame, and hatred for (whoever this applies to).

I repent on behalf of myself as well as for my ancestors for any generational iniquity and ungodly spiritual practices. As I stand before you as a blood-bought Christian, I ask you to take the blood of Christ to my ancestral bloodline and cleanse iniquity right back through the generations to Adam and Eve and by your blood, cleanse those who are alive and remain today, in Jesus Name. Please now render a verdict from your courtroom that all these things that the enemy has stolen must be restored".

The following summary is a guideline for some of the areas that we may need to pray for:

- trauma of abuse and displacement, (being taken from our family/community group, traditions)
- the spirit of captivity,
- grief from being dispossessed and marginalized, mistreated, and diminished.
- victim mentality, self-pity, shame, rejection, abandonment,
- powerlessness, orphan spirit, poverty mentality
- loss of identity and purpose, hopelessness, despair
- Substance abuse and addictive spirits
- Sexual violation, incest, rape
- Immorality – fornication, adultery, pedophilia
- Violence, abuse
- Anger
- Fear
- Bitterness
- Shame, blaming others
- Ancestral spiritual practices (negative soul ties to those family forebears that have perpetuated these)
- Pride
- Ungodly domination and control
- Generational sickness, or physical weaknesses
- Theft, dishonesty
- Trauma from war experiences
- Loss of initiative

We can ask the Holy Spirit to reveal anything that needs to be confessed, repented of, renounced, and broken off. Often, we don't know everything from our past, but we can apply the blood of Christ to cleanse and heal the known and unknown wounds and iniquity from the DNA of our ancestral line, ourselves, our children, and their offspring. We must break off stronghold spirits of destruction attached to all the bloodlines breaking soul ties and agreement with them.

We then ask the Spirit of God to heal and recalibrate all the areas of negative programming and to heal our memories. This cleansing and healing of the memories must be applied to the soul as well as the cellular memories of our neurological pathways as this is vital to recovery. There needs to be a reset of the brain itself from the effects of trauma and in the spirit of our minds (Eph. 4:23) to embrace the newness of identity and life.

We need to ask the Spirit of God to 'initialize' or activate those areas that have been crushed and deactivated and to restore a sense of dignity, identity, initiative, and self-worth that is based on our relationship with Him.

It can bring great healing if the leaders of a nation that enslaved, mistreated, or displaced another cultural group acknowledge the wrong that they did to that nation. However, if this does not happen, freedom still belongs to those who have accepted Christ as Saviour and have come into His new kingdom, forgiving the past and releasing those who harmed them to God.

A powerful key for healing and restoration of any cultural group is when their leaders will stand up and take account for all their own generational iniquity and dysfunction and when they lead their people to forgive those who sinned against them as a nation. Whether on an individual or corporate level, we must all repent for our own unforgiveness towards those who hurt us, no matter how hard that is. This breaks every curse associated with our history.

What happened back then wasn't right, it wasn't our fault, it wasn't fair, but how we deal with it now will either perpetuate that cycle of destruction or release healing and restoration to those present and to future generations.

CHAPTER TWENTY-FOUR

Regional Spirits

As mentioned earlier, Isaiah 51:1 tells us that we are to *"look to the rock from which we were hewn and the pit from which we came"*, to see if there is anything specific in our foundations that needs to be dealt with. This doesn't just refer to our immediate family bloodline, but it can also refer to our cultural inheritance.

Sometimes it is as simple a thing as a passive spirit, a 'she'll be right' mentality that can make us apathetic in life and in our walk with God. This attitude can be over nations and is often attributed to Australia and New Zealand. We are not meant to just try to change a passive attitude if its roots are generational, but rather we must look to where it came from and deal with it in the power of the Spirit. We can all look back and see where we have ungodly issues or attitudes that have been traits within our parents or grandparents that relate to their cultural inheritance.

One instance in the Bible that speaks of regional, territorial spirits is in the book of Daniel. Daniel had a troubling prophetic dream. He had been seeking God in prayer for some time and had not yet seen the answer to his petition. Eventually, an angel appeared to him one day to bring the answer to his prayer, and he explained the delay.

> Daniel 10:12-14 (NIV) *"Then he continued, "Do not be afraid, Daniel. Since the first day that you set your mind to gain understanding and to humble yourself before your God, your words were heard, and I have come in response to them. 13 But the prince of the Persian kingdom resisted me twenty-one days. Then Michael, one of the chief princes, came to help me, because I was detained there with the king of Persia. 14 Now I have come to explain to you what will happen to your people in the future, for the vision concerns a time yet to come."*

Although God had dispatched His angelic messenger from the outset as Daniel began to pray, there was a battle in the heavens with the regional spirits that caused a delay in Daniel receiving the answer to his prayer.

You will notice how nations that were founded in Christianity have far more prosperity, fair government, respect for women, and a greater sense of humanity than some other nations. You also see that as adherence to Christianity has declined in our nations that we have more social problems, drug addiction, and violence within our land. When our nations' leaders legalise things that are not in alignment with God's word, will, and purpose, they open the heavens to the ungodly spirit realm, and this brings oppression upon its people.

Ungodly spiritual strongholds over nations may include poverty, child sex trade, oppression of women, apathy, genocide, drug cartel strongholds, and many other things. Ungodly spiritual beliefs and practices open the door to demonic powers that will remain over those regions to bring oppression to those who live there. While we have the authority to take Christ's blood to our own generational issues, most teachers on this subject believe that only a person with the authority of an apostolic anointing should try to deal with regional, territorial spirits.

Understanding generational influences

"We have been shaped by what we have 'come out of'. It is impossible not to be.

We are shaped by the country, the history of the country, and the country's culture that we have come out of.

For instance, as a young man raised in Northern Ireland, I joined the Orange Order. Had I been born and raised in Denmark, or India, I would never have joined that organisation because it plays no part whatsoever in their culture. Rather the culture of those countries would then have shaped me substantially.

Worship leader Carl Tuttle put it well when he said, "There is nothing wrong with our culture unless it clashes with the culture of the Kingdom of God". **https://chris-tian-restoration.com/understanding_generational_issues. htm**

A while back, I was mentoring a young single woman from New Zealand who had had extremely poor foundations in her childhood which were not just relevant to her immediate family but also her cultural background. She had been a drug user in the past and had two little boys to two different fathers. She had become a Christian and was deeply passionate in her walk with God and was very dedicated to being a good mother to her boys. One day as I was praying with her, I felt to pray for her bloodline for the desolation of generations where ancestors had failed to nurture each successive generation parentally. I took the blood of Christ to the 'orphan spirit', areas of desolation and loss of identity and validation. I saw this young woman about a week later and she said to me, "I had a call from my mother on the weekend after you prayed for me, and she apologized for not nurturing me when I was growing up". This had been a very healing experience for her.

Another instance that comes back to me was a young man I prayed for in my church. He had asked me for some ministry, so I did some generational prayer over his bloodline and began to pray about some other issues in his life, but then I felt led to go back to his bloodline and break the spirit of poverty over him generationally. After I finished praying, he said, "That was awesome that you picked up the 'poverty spirit'. The place where I grew up in New Zealand was named Poverty Bay".

Conclusion

Whatever our cultural background or our childhood foundations consisted of God has a plan for us. He is the God who makes all things new. Thankfully, He knows everything about us, and our history and he desires to restore all that has been taken from us (Joel 2:22).

> *"In Japan, broken objects are often repaired with gold. The flaw is seen as a unique piece of the object's history, which adds to its beauty. Consider this when you feel broken"* **http://homewithheart.com/cardshop2/in-japan-broken-objects-are-often-repaired-with-gold**

There are so many promises in the word of God about restoration and restitution. God is a just God and desires to recompense us for all the troubles of our past. When God restores us, He makes us better than new. He promises in Isaiah 61:7-8: (KJV)

> *"For your shame ye shall have double; and for confusion they shall rejoice in their portion: therefore in their land they shall possess the double: everlasting joy shall be unto them. 8 For I the Lord love judgment, I hate robbery for*

burnt offering; and I will direct their work in truth, and I will make an everlasting covenant with them".

God has redeemed us through the precious blood of His Son. There was no higher price that He could pay to restore us to Himself and to adopt us as His children.

1 John 3:1 (NIV) *"See what great love the Father has lavished on us, that we should be called children of God! And that is what we are! The reason the world does not know us is that it did not know him".*

He wants to heal and deliver us from our past and restore us to wholeness, then in turn to use us to bring others into His kingdom and into His wholeness.

Isaiah 43:18-21 (NIV) *"Forget the former things; do not dwell on the past. 19 See, I am doing a new thing! Now it springs up; do you not perceive it? I am making a way in the wilderness and streams in the wasteland. 20 The wild animals honor me, the jackals and the owls, because I provide water in the wilderness and streams in the wasteland, to give drink to my people, my chosen, 21 the people I formed for myself that they may proclaim my praise".*

I believe that we are entering into a season of restoration and acceleration where God is quickening restoration to His people. We must play our part by staying on track with Him. We must keep following the leading of His Spirit or otherwise, if we walk in our own ways, we will just continue to open doors to the enemy to bring destruction. He is an amazing God and He has not forgotten you.

Isaiah 49:15-25 (NIV) *"Can a mother forget the baby at her breast and have no compassion on the child she has borne? Though she may forget, I will not forget you!*

16 See, I have engraved you on the palms of my hands; your walls are ever before me.

17 Your children hasten back, and those who laid you waste depart from you.

18 Lift up your eyes and look around; all your children gather and come to you. As surely as I live," declares the Lord, "you will wear them all as ornaments; you will put them on, like a bride.

19 "Though you were ruined and made desolate and your land laid waste, now you will be too small for your people, and those who devoured you will be far away.

20 The children born during your bereavement will yet say in your hearing, 'This place is too small for us; give us more space to live in.'

21 Then you will say in your heart, 'Who bore me these? I was bereaved and barren; I was exiled and rejected. Who brought these up? I was left all alone, but these—where have they come from?'"

22 This is what the Sovereign Lord says: "See, I will beckon to the nations, I will lift up my banner to the peoples; they will bring your sons in their arms and carry your daughters on their hips.

23 Kings will be your foster fathers, and their queens your nursing mothers. They will bow down before you with their faces to the ground; they will lick the dust at your feet. Then you will know that I am the Lord; those who hope in me will not be disappointed."

24 Can plunder be taken from warriors, or captives be rescued from the fierce?

25 But this is what the Lord says: "Yes, captives will be taken from warriors, and plunder retrieved from the fierce; I will contend with those who contend with you, and your children I will save".

9 798989 502615